15 Shifts

The essential guide to transform your talent management

JoAnn R. Corley

15 Shifts | The essential guide to transform your talent
management

Written by: JoAnn R. Corley

To order this book visit www.thehumansphere.com
All rights reserved.
ISBN: 1507875878
ISBN-13: 978-1507875872

Dedicated to all who have an unflinching commitment to the stewardship of those they lead.
JoAnn Corley

▭ CONTENTS

Preface.

This is not your typical business book. Consider this a combination of a conversation and a handbook or reference guide – both simple and practical so you can take immediate action. Used as created, it can be your blueprint for building a profitable talent management infrastructure.

It begins with a story about an advisor and key leader conducting a series of meetings to assess the state of a company. Through these meetings the advisor guides the leader through a progression of mental shifts as they uncover the leader's true desires for the company and ultimate leadership footprint.

Those shifts are essential in executing the changes needed to successfully fulfill those desires.

In reality, it could be the story of any leader. It could be your story or other key leaders within your organization.

Additionally, it's not a story of a company doing so terrible it's desperate for help, but rather one who is, at first look, doing well and therefore initially sees itself with little need for improvement.

And that's what makes the story and this handbook so important.

Beyond the conversation, as the book continues, additional shifts are revealed. Please know, without any of the shifts, you're company is less profitable. In fact it's probably losing money. To help you determine whether that's true for you, we'll cover how to calculate that and the level of ROI attainable if you choose to incorporate these shifts in your leadership thinking and business practices.

One final note: don't let the size of this handbook fool you. It's small but powerful – chock full of information on how you can substantially impact your bottom-line, leadership and career.

Let's get started...

"Great vision without great people is irrelevant."
- Jim Collins

Introduction.

Over the years I've had the opportunity to hear a breath of stories from managers, individual contributors and leaders regarding their desire and attempt to successfully leed and be lead.

After conducting professional development workshops throughout North America, I feel as if I've heard it all – successful stories *and* epic failures. Those workshops resulted in thousands of interactions over the years and provided me with a unique perspective on common challenges in the workplace today, the majority of which can be traced to leadership and people management practices.

The stories all seem to have recurring themes – particularly the troubling stories. During each conversation I would ask the same series of questions. Many of the answers were the same:

What kind of management training do you have? *Very little.*

Why don't you fire that person? *We can't – HR is afraid we'll get sued.*

How do you track the performance or document the behavior of that employee? *We don't, we just do annual performance reviews… and you know how those go.*

Why hasn't the 'bully' manager been fired? *It seems like upper management just doesn't care – and we've talked to HR and they can't seem to do anything.*

Those statements above are actual answers. I have a laundry list of responses and they all carry similar themes related to an incomplete and sorely inadequate approach to managing talent. The answers are what drove me to create this handbook.

This handbook couples a short tale surrounded with critical yet easy-to-use information on how to establish a comprehensive talent management infrastructure.

> My goal is to make it as easy as possible for leaders and decision-makers in any size company to generate greater company profits through effective talent management.

So who is this book for? Aside from HR professionals (we'll call you internal consultants!) at any level of their career, this book is also for leaders looking to increase their organizational effectiveness.

HR Professionals
Though certification programs are useful and important in a human resource career building strategy, this handbook affordably and quickly shortens the learning curve for the overarching purpose of any human resource department – talent management. *You can be highly certified and yet not be a competent talent management practitioner. I see it all the time.* I believe being a skilled talent management practitioner is a must.

Leaders & Key Decision-Makers
It's a new day in talent management and if it's to be the most effective, everyone needs to understand it and see their role in it. Successful talent management extends way beyond the Human Resource Department all the way to the C-suite. Why? Talent Management is a crucial element of business strategy. Clearly strategy cannot be executed without people. The better the talent is managed the better the strategy is executed. It's such a simple concept and though widely acknowledged, it's not broadly practiced.

Pivotal Benefits – The 15 Shifts
You'll quickly notice that a significant and consistent theme throughout this book is "change must occur" and identifies specifically where.

The Shifts help to identify and describe those changes -- to what levels and in what ways. It suggests that successful, comprehensive changes within an organization can only occur when key leaders first change themselves – initially and most importantly in their thinking -- so that they can effectively lead others to do the same. It's tough to take someone where you've not been yourself or are unwilling to go.

You'll glean from this book that many shifts must occur to get from Point A to Point B and ultimately to success.

I see these critical shifts in two primary categories:

1) Foundational shifts which garner the thinking and understanding to even see the need and want to make the changes.

Examples of areas where these types of shifts may occur:
- How leadership/decision-makers value employees
- Leaderships' sensitivity to what employees need
- Understanding the talent management ripple affect and its revenue impact
- Money invested will bring a substantial return (ultimately, it's not an expense but investment)
- Talent management is not optional, but should be a standard element of any business strategy

2) Shifts when implementing the essential components of talent management. For this to occur, operational processes and the people involved may need to change.

Examples:
- Managers at all levels incorporating talent management practices within their roles.
- Management training being a non-negotiable component to a strong talent management infrastructure.
- Changing how employee training is seen and used
- Using performance software as a coaching tool

No change can occur unless there is first a shift in thinking or feeling that can then impact other components in decision-making.

Each shift serves as a building block in forming a solid, cohesive, profitable talent management infrastructure.

This is a key human behavior insight – people won't change until what they think or how they feel changes first.

So for all of you internal consultants (my fellow HR compadres) reading this book, please know verbal acknowledgement of needed changes do not mean that change will come. There needs to be a change on the inside for change to occur on the outside. **I call the changes on the inside -- *shifts*.**

In a broader context, when thinking about leaders altering elements of a business, and when many stakeholders are involved, *many shifts* need to occur before change can be realized and cemented.

As you read this book, you'll see examples of shifts such as: knowledge, beliefs, values, desires, thinking, motivation, emotions and resource allocation, to name a few. Use these as your guide. Train yourself to identify these within your organization and in a conversation. These are the necessary identifiers or shifts that must be in place.

Remember, change feels hard when it's forced or coerced because the internal shifts have not occurred. If the shifts have not occurred, resistance will be present and the more substantial the change, the stronger the resistance will be.

As a side note, this human behavior truth applies to coaching employees as well. Where there is resistance, there probably have not been the necessary internal shifts.

How to Use This Book

First, let it educate you. Then identify what's the quickest way you can take action to get something started.

Additionally, use this book...
- ✓ To assess who else needs to read it and make sure they get a copy!
- ✓ In staff meetings
- ✓ As a component of strategic planning sessions
- ✓ As a continuous resource and reference guide
- ✓ If you're an internal consultant (as all HR professionals are), use it as a springboard to provide thought leadership by writing an executive briefing
- ✓ To make a commitment to become a wildly successful talent management practitioner
- ✓ To track your progress
- ✓ To measure results financially
- ✓ And give me feedback and ask questions

It's contents will save you time and years of people management trial and error by suggesting the most important areas to which to give your precious attention. That strategic attention will provide the quickest and most substantial return on investment.

"To win in the marketplace you must first win in the workplace." - Doug Conant

Section I
The Conversation

The Story

It begins with you and me, a newly acquired advisor, sitting together at the local coffee shop conducting a status discussion about your business.

|> Shift #1
I can have talent management needs even if my company is doing well. My company can go from good to great or pain to recovery.

The Coffee Shop

We begin our time together with informal introductions. You're a key decision-maker reflecting on your business' success to date.

You believe you have many things right –in fact, things are going well. You have good processes in place, a solid, loyal customer base poised for continued growth, a great product, a strong brand identity and for the most part you are satisfied with the company's revenue numbers over the past few years.

As you continue your assessment, you recall a quote from a book you read several years back titled *Good to Great* by Jim Collins, "Good is the enemy of great," you share. To you that message seemed profound and continues to resonate with you.

You pause for a moment, looking off into the distance. As a coach and advisor, I've seen that look many times before. That's the look that suggests something isn't quite right.

You catch yourself, quickly apologize for drifting off and then continue, "You know, we're good - but we're not great. I want great!"

As our discussion moves along, a young woman stopping by the table to say hello briefly interrupts us. At first you don't recognize her, but as she reveals her name and expresses a hearty hello, your memory is jogged.

After a cordial exchange and a pleasant goodbye I ask, "Who is she?"
You reply, "She's a very talented employee who left our company several years ago."

"Why did she leave?" I ask.

With a tone of curiosity you respond, "I don't know... really. But when I noticed she was gone, I felt a bit of disappointment because I understood her to be one of our best."

Curious myself, I continue the inquiry, "Why don't you know? If it bothered you, even just a bit, why didn't you find out the circumstance of her leaving?"

You chuckle, "Come on... I've got a lot going on. If I pursued every little issue related to our employees I'd get nothing done."

My probing persists, "Well, you mentioned she's talented and you lost her. Is that a little issue? Isn't that a loss worth knowing about?"

With slight annoyance you reply, "Hey, really... it's not my job to keep track of every single employee."

"Ok, for the moment, fair enough," I say. I'm a bit surprised at how quickly the issue is dismissed. It reflects an interesting line of thinking I know I need to explore and an absence of a value I know successful business leaders need to have.

At this point, I realize I now have to fully possess my advisor role and continue the inquiry knowing full well you might see it more as an interrogation rather than an inquiry.

"How about this," I start, "Is it part of your role to keep track of profit and loss?"

Now appearing a bit more irked, you shrugged your shoulders and spouted, "Of course." I could see the look of "dah" in your demeanor.

I continue, "Well, how much did it cost you -- how much loss did you incur when this talented employee left?"

"What do you mean?" you ask.

"Every action of your employees impacts your company operations and ultimately your revenue in both tangible and intangible ways. In essence, having a talented employee leave has a negative impact on your revenue from lost productivity, costs associated with replacement – you know, turnover costs."

"Well of course, theoretically everyone knows that," you respond.

I pause, then respond, "So... how much?"

Frown lines begin to appear as you take a sip of coffee. Leaning back in your chair, with a deep long sigh you reply, "Frankly, I have no idea."

I can tell that the tone of your response resembles a cup of 'I'm annoyed you're asking me', with a shot of 'I think I probably should know this but don't', dashed with a pinch of 'why don't I know this', topped off with 'gee, what's the number and does it really matter?'

I wait for a moment. I want whatever impact this conversation is having within you to be had. This is the tough part of what I do – moving clients to a place of discomfort in the spirit of facilitating needed change for their highest good.

I know that allowing impact fuels authentic change; that hearing the truth and then wrestling with it is the alchemy leaders need for personal growth to be truly effective. When that occurs, a leader can then translate that personal growth into company growth.

You see, *people* lead companies, and their leadership is influenced by who they are on the inside. Personal growth is professional growth.

I also know that when talent leaves a company and key decision makers don't know why, don't know how much it's costing them, and don't know the connection between talent and business strategy (and ultimately company success), there needs to be a change – a *shift* needs to occur.

That shift needs to occur holistically; in thinking, values, philosophy and emotions, enough to drive different decisions that result in substantial, meaningful action.

I decided to end the wait. "You know, it's been my experience that many leaders don't know the answers to the questions I just asked," I said, "That's what keeps me in business."

You chuckle, taking a deep breath with a grin.

I go on, "And that's probably the ultimate reason why we're meeting today, though you would not have described it in these terms. I'd like to suggest that your desire to take your company from good to great resides substantially in the arena of how your employees are managed from start to finish."

"I suspect that if you did a people management audit so to speak, you'd find areas of need that directly impact your company's profit and which have undermined your company's ability to move from good to great."

"And finally," I continue, "And this is the most difficult to see because your company is doing well, these issues that have a negative impact really seem of little consequence and therefore are treated lightly or with complete indifference; an example of which is not knowing or even being motivated to know why your talent leaves."

"Hum," you quietly reply. Your brows raise, your eyes widen and your head begins to nod as you slowly say, "And therein is a perfect example of good being the enemy of great."

Little did you know, that quote is also one of my favorites! In my work, it's not very hard to acquire a client whose people management practices are causing obvious destruction to a business. The house is obviously on fire and the fire department is called.

What's more difficult is to offer help to a client when in most areas competent leadership is demonstrated resulting in a successful company that has positive revenue results. The house appears perfectly in tact, is functioning well and little attention is paid to the space heater next to the flammable chemicals.

As any wise person would tell you, success in some or even most areas does not mean automatic success in all areas.

In my experience, *good is also the anesthetic to great.* It numbs us to what's possible, to what isn't working and to the changes needed that are obvious to the non-anesthetized.

They begin to notice when the pain starts to appear as the anesthesia begins losing its effect. That's when they call me.

I look up and say, "We are meeting today to see how your company can go from good to great rather than pain to recovery. One takes much more effort, time and money. I'm sure you know which. *Assessing your good helps you avoid risking the good.*"

There's a significant moment of silence.

"No offense," you exclaim, "but I could leave right now and begin to make changes and I haven't paid you a dime! I'm a big fan of free you know."

I laughed. "Yes, that has happened. A competent advisor can provide value even in one conversation. I've experienced that myself when seeking help. So yes, you could do that."

"But my sense is you see this conversation as a catalyst to jumpstart your efforts to great, knowing that it will take more than one conversation."

We both smiled. Continuing to chat, we finished our coffee knowing the first and most significant hurdle had been crossed. *The first shift* had successfully occurred.

The next step... *the shift* being tested. Would it hold? That was yet to be determined.

Meeting in Your Office

It's been a couple of weeks since our initial conversation at the coffee shop. You've gone back to the reality of your day-to-day responsibilities, lingering are the insights from our initial meeting.

During those couple of weeks, you've shared elements of our conversation with a few close colleagues and friends. You've discovered there are a few who believe that too much emphasis on employees reflected weakened leadership and presented opportunities to be taken advantage of. One of the questions some colleagues asked, "What if you invest more time and money and they leave? Wouldn't that be a waste?
You thought to yourself that argument makes so much sense. We function on such a tight budget and margin as it is.

On the other hand one of your more enlightened colleagues known for being "forward thinking" and whose company has been progressively successful even during the economic downturn posed this response, "What if you invest in them and they stay -- longer?"

In spite of the conflicting input, most agreed that taking the time to look closely at what was happening on the on "people side" of the business needed to occur.

You initiated our next meeting and along with sharing the results of your many conversations, expressed curiosity as to what the process would be and what exactly would be uncovered.

I walk into your company entrance and it seems bright and cheery. The receptionist is pleasant and professional. She says you were expecting me and pointed to a long hallway.

As I make my way through the corridor, it leads me to the back part of the building. I pass many rows of cubicles and the atmosphere seems slightly subdued. When I encounter an employee and exchange greetings there is a friendly, yet controlled response.

I finally make my way to your office in the back of the building. Captured by the beautiful view of the woods through the windows lining the back wall. I exclaim, "It feels wonderfully calm and peaceful. What a great office!"

You greet me warmly with a hearty handshake and reply, "Yes, isn't it! I spend a lot of time in here."

Your warmth is a good sign. So far, *the shift* seems to have held.

I open our meeting, "It's good to see you again. I was pleased that you shared the results of your discussions with your colleagues and friends, both supportive and not and I'm glad you have chosen to move forward."

"Honestly," you reply, "The more the insights of our conversation settled, the more compelled I felt to act."

This is a very good sign for me as it reflects that our conversation had more than a superficial impact. I know that when any initiative of this nature needs to occur it must be whole-heartedly endorsed and supported by all key stakeholders and decision-makers. You were the beginning. Someone has to lead the charge.

"So," you continue, "Where do we begin?"

"We're going to start with a few preliminary questions for you and your key leadership team. I recommend each person initially answer independently. For our meeting today, I'd like to use these questions to guide our discussion.

But before we proceed with the questions, I'd like to offer some thoughts on how we will language our activity moving forward and why."

|> Shift #2
How You See Them & What You Call Them Matters

There has been an evolution of terms used to describe employees throughout the history of commerce. In the industrial age they were referred to as laborers or workers.

As compensation evolved so did the labels - from laborer to salary man and the evolution has continued. We now have an assortment of labels such as team members, associates, and staff all in the spirit of reflecting their status as well as how they are seen or valued.

Additionally, as business and leadership models have continued to change, so has the perceived relationship between leaders and employees. For many companies it's seen more as a collaborative partnership rather than a "do as I say" command and control-relating style.

As workplaces became more sophisticated, along with the arrival of the knowledge worker, individual employees (individual contributors) have become more empowered. Flatten hierarchies and the need for more specialized skills continued to enhance their status. It seems as if an employee's sense of value has evolved and with that what we call them.

The word employee seems to be a more legal term these days. For many companies, individual contributor or talent is becoming a more popular descriptor.

I like the term talent because it carries and reflects the weight of the impact to a company. Consider the following phrases:

> *"managing employees"*
> *"managing people"*
> *"managing workers"*
> *"managing talent"*

For me each phrase carries a different sensibility. It may not be the same feel for everyone, in my view, *managing talent* sounds more hopeful, upbeat, important, and evokes a greater sense of responsibility from all parties.

The Discussion Continues

"So, for our work together, I'd like to call it talent management. Will you agree to this language?"

With a thoughtful look you reply, "Yes I do. It does have a different ring to it."

I invite you to step into the doorway of your office and look out onto the open work area of your staff and say the following, "There is talent here. It's that talent that successfully runs this company and I want to effectively manage it. I am a talent manager, I am *their* talent manager."

As you walk back to the round meeting table, you smile with what seemed to be a newfound satisfaction. I smiled as well. I knew another *shift* had just occurred.

You agreed to shift your sense of value towards your employees by calling them something that carries more meaning. *You decided to elevate your relationship with them and your sense of responsibility to them.*

As we settled back into our chairs, leaning forward on your elbows you say, "I know without a doubt, from this time forward, this business and I will have a better year than we had last and our work has just begun."

"Isn't it amazing how addressing our thinking and philosophies alone can impact our results?" I asked. "Each shift is a building block, paving the way to the next stage of your success."

All Aboard

"Before I leave," I continued, "I do need to present you with one more question. When it comes time to survey your leadership team, do you believe each of them holds the beliefs and attitudes to which you've now shifted?"

"Hmm...that's a good question."

I go on, "Yes, in fact that's an essential question. Good to great is not a singular achievement by one person alone, but a combination of philosophy, processes, practices and resources held and used by *all stakeholders* with committed leadership advancing the charge."

"Of course, of course, I see what you mean." You take a deep breath.

"I don't have the complete answer to your question, but what I do have is a clearer understanding that more will be required of my leadership than what I first imagined. If I want my company to be different, I will need to be different too. I will need to be the kind of leader that can influence and execute change in a much more significant way than I have in the past. I plainly see, a different company requires different leadership."

"You are sounding wiser by the minute," I say. "Now you're ready to dive into your questions."

|> Shift #3
A different company will require different leadership. If I want my company to change, then I will need to change – first.

|> Shift #4
Effective talent management can only be executed if all leaders are on board... and they too have made the shifts.

The Initial Review

"I call these questions a Talent Management review or audit. Eventually we'll be conducting it with all your key leaders, but first we'll start with just you and I.

I'd like for you to take reflective time, being thorough and authentic in your answers. There is no judgment here; it's not a test. These questions begin the process of shaping your talent management thinking and philosophy, while identifying what's in place that's been useful and also revealing what might be missing.

This is about continuing to build a firm foundation for all activity moving forward.

You'll start with the Part 1 questions, then review the Holistic Talent Management Map and finish with answering the questions in Part 2.

I'll head out now. Let's plan on meeting next week."

It's Your Turn
Let's take a break from the story. Has anything resonated so far?...anything you can relate to? And the most important question -- have you made any shifts?

Let's review the four revealed thus far:

|> Shift #1
I can have talent management needs even if my company is doing well. My company can go from good to great or pain to recovery.

|> Shift #2
How you see them and what you call them matters. How you value them is how you'll treat them.

|> Shift #3
A different company will require different leadership. If I want my company to change, then I will need to change – first.

|> Shift #4
Effective talent management can only be executed if all leaders are on board... and they too have made the shifts.

Here's your chance as the reader to begin your own audit in whatever way is applicable to you. This is a guidebook. It's meant and designed to prompt you to action. Plan on gaining results!

Talent Management Review - Preliminary Audit

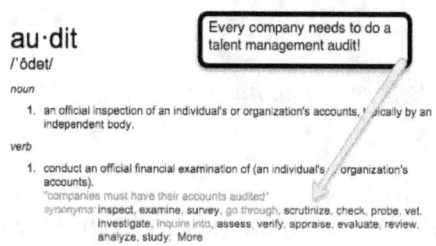

au·dit
/'ôdet/

noun
1. an official inspection of an individual's or organization's accounts, typically by an independent body.

verb
1. conduct an official financial examination of (an individual's / organization's accounts).
"companies must have their accounts audited"
synonyms: inspect, examine, survey, go through, scrutinize, check, probe, vet, investigate, inquire into, assess, verify, appraise, evaluate, review, analyze, study. More

Every company needs to do a talent management audit!

PART 1.

1. What is **your** definition of talent management; what does it look like to you?

2. Do you have a personal talent management philosophy and if so, what is it?

3. What is your belief regarding the connection between talent management and it's financial impact?

4. If you believe it makes an impact, are you able to quantify it (calculate it)?

5. How are you currently executing (expressing, demonstrating) talent management within your organization?
    Here are 4 contexts to get you started...
    activities
    processes

tools
resources

6. What do you think you are doing well?
    If asked, would the majority of your employees agree?

7. What do you think you are not doing well / identify areas
    of improvement?
    How would your employees answer this question?

8. Depending on how you answered questions 6 & 7, what's
    the financial impact -- how much do you think it's
    costing or saving you annually?

Next, let's look at the **Talent Management Strategy Map.** Take
some time and review each segment. Here's where you can fine-
tune your answers. Consider that your answers can be
converted into an action plan.

Following the map, you'll notice the items on the map have been
provided in a list format. You may find it easier after reviewing
the map to use the list to make notes.

A Holistic Talent Management Map

A Strategic Planning Guide

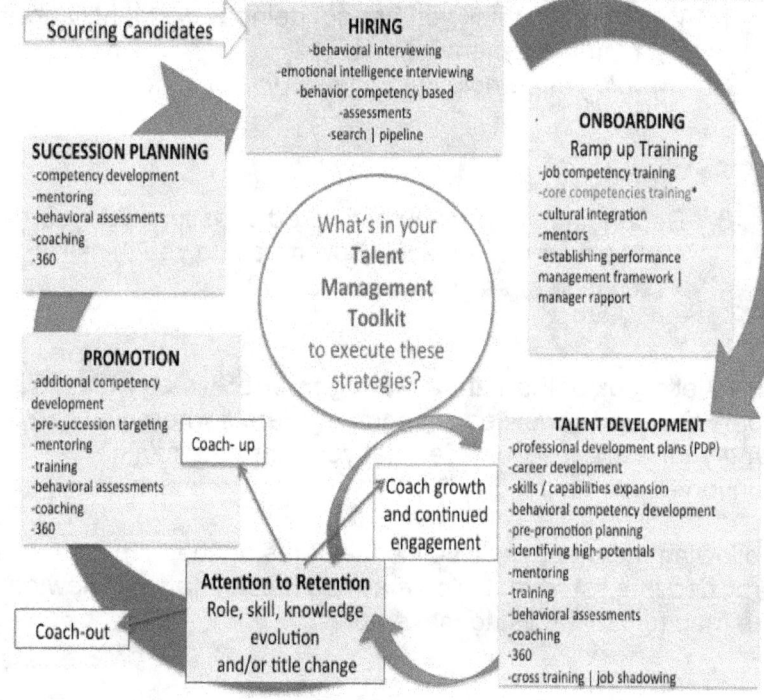

Holistic Talent Management: Life Cycle of An Employee

Sourcing Candidates

HIRING
-behavioral interviewing
-emotional intelligence interviewing
-behavior competency based
-assessments
-search | pipeline

ONBOARDING
Ramp up Training
-job competency training
-core competencies training*
-cultural integration
-mentors
-establishing performance management framework | manager rapport

SUCCESSION PLANNING
-competency development
-mentoring
-behavioral assessments
-coaching
-360

What's in your **Talent Management Toolkit** to execute these strategies?

PROMOTION
-additional competency development
-pre-succession targeting
-mentoring
-training
-behavioral assessments
-coaching
-360

Coach- up

Coach growth and continued engagement

TALENT DEVELOPMENT
-professional development plans (PDP)
-career development
-skills / capabilities expansion
-behavioral competency development
-pre-promotion planning
-identifying high-potentials
-mentoring
-training
-behavioral assessments
-coaching
-360
-cross training | job shadowing

Attention to Retention
Role, skill, knowledge evolution and/or title change

Coach-out

Talent Management Review - Preliminary Audit

PART 2.

Review the comprehensive map provided – Diagram 1

What do you need/want to incorporate?

Why? (What would be the benefits?)

What current challenges would it address?

What would be the positive financial impact?

In what areas do you need to increase your knowledge?

Taking into account your answers from Part 1 and Part 2,

> Where are the bright spots of your talent management practices?

>What would you say are your most significant needs?

After you have recorded your answer(s), rate them from most significant to least significant - **1** being **most**, 5 being **least**

Holistic Talent Management – Strategic Planning Checklist
(extracted from the complete map - add more of your own where applicable)

Stage 1: HIRING
- Behavioral interviewing
- Emotional intelligence interviewing
- Behavior competency based
- Assessments
- Search / pipeline

Stage 2: ONBOARDING
(includes "ramp up training")
- Job competency training
- Individual contributor core competencies training*
[personal branding, time management, collaboration, creative-critical thinking, emotional intelligence, business writing]
- Cultural (company, team) integration
- Mentors
- Establishing performance management framework / manager rapport

Stage 3: TALENT DEVELOPMENT
(and Attention to Retention)
Role, skill, knowledge development: evolution of role and/or title change / pre-promotion preparation | coach up, coach out, coach growth and continued engagement
- Professional development plans (PDP)
- Career development
- Skills / capabilities expansion
- Behavioral competency development
- Pre-promotion planning
- Identifying high-potentials
- Mentoring
- Training
- Behavioral assessments

- Coaching
- 360 Review
- Cross training
- Job shadowing

Stage 4: PROMOTION
- Additional competency development
- Pre-succession targeting
- Mentoring
- Training
- Behavioral assessments
- Coaching
- 360 Review

Stage 5: SUCCESSION PLANNING
- Competency development
- Mentoring
- Behavioral assessments
- Coaching
- 360 Review

Notes ✐

|> Shift #5
Talent management is a comprehensive integrated business strategy

Now that you've worked through the "audit", I wonder if you got the feeling I did when I first designed it. For me it felt as if I was working through the operations of a business. You may have envisioned certain people in particular roles, how they performed, what they where like to manage, etc.

These and more had an impact on how quickly, easily, efficiently or effectively your overall business strategy was executed and goals that were or were not met.

We cannot separate people from the process. The kind of talent you have will dictate the success level of any strategy, vision, plan or goal. I know that sounds terribly obvious and overly simplistic, yet if we *look closely* at the attitudes, philosophies and practices of many decision-makers regarding talent management, you'll notice that decisions are made as if this was true! It's as if a fog of denial clouds the operational sensibilities regarding this area of the business.

The reason, I believe, is leaders really don't know what to do with it – don't feel competent in this arena, so they act as if it doesn't matter, minimizing its importance.

Look at the list you reviewed, daunting even to those who've been human resource professionals for sometime. There is a lot that goes into managing people effectively and aligning these efforts to profitably support business operations. It's way beyond administrative paperwork. And that's why even many HR professionals are struggling to meet the needs of their company in this area.

"If you only have a hammer, you'll see everything as a nail."
- Abraham Maslow

|> SHIFT #6
Talent management requires a toolkit of resources to fulfill its objectives

I love that quote! Imagine a builder attempting to construct a house with only a hammer. Ridiculous, yes? That's what many companies attempt to do, build and manage a resource of talent with few, if any tools.

To be the most effective, you need to be the most equipped. In the case of talent management, you need a toolkit – a collection of resources to successfully execute your talent management strategy and construct your talent management infrastructure.

Infrastructure Matters
Some have no infrastructure at all. When I think of infrastructure, I imagine the vast connection of highways throughout our country. I can't even imagine what it was like before these highways were built -- driving or even attempting to get from let's say Connecticut to Illinois on a dirt or gravel road or even the prairie grass!

The value and purpose of a highway infrastructure, for example, is to support, provide ease of operation, provide meaningful, useful connections, provide efficiency, safety and ultimately accomplish the desired outcome of getting from point A to point B – quicker, better, faster.

I remember when a major bridge on highway I-35 in Minneapolis-St. Paul collapsed several years back. During its repair, it disrupted traffic for quite a while. It was and still is a significant connector for the Twin Cities infrastructure. Without it, there was wasted time, inconvenience and more money spent on commuting as well as repairs.

That bridge demonstrates that each component in an infrastructure serves a critical role. Without them, its designed cannot be fully realized.

The same is true in talent management. Rather than having a well thought out, planned and constructed infrastructure to most effectively support managing their precious human resource, many companies opt for no infrastructure but rather the ad hoc or buffet style approach. I'll take a little bit of this and a little bit of that. Oh this looks good, I'll grab something from over here and certainly this must be good because it looks so wonderful. And before you know it, they are at the checkout station dishing out oodles of cash assuming it's all going to taste yummy and be incredibly satisfying.

Needless to say, lots of time and money are wasted with this approach even though a few items on the plate might taste good and even yield mild results. And it's the mild results that get us. We might be lulled into thinking this is it without ever coming to know there is so much more and it's so much better!

Behavioral assessments are a great example of this. They are so affordable and offer so much needed assistance when selecting the best candidate to hire or promote. We'll talk more about assessments later.

Building the Infrastructure – Your Talent Management Toolkit

To build your infrastructure, you'll need equipment and tools. With this in mind, I've provided below a *starter list* of recommended categories, resources and tools to have in your talent management toolkit. There may be others you'll want to add that are unique to your industry.

As with any toolbox or kit, these items should be available to use as needed and also should be used appropriately, with wisdom and in conjunction with other elements of the talent management infrastructure. For example, a component of the infrastructure is *"attention to retention"*. A tool in your toolkit is an employee survey. Don't plan on doing an employee survey if you have no intention of responding to the results.

Another example -- some companies spend a tremendous amount of money on employee rewards programs, but little on training their managers who may have behaviors that undermine the intention and desired outcomes of the reward program.

These examples reinforce the point that *full commitment* is needed to every aspect of the Talent Management Map to realize its maximum benefits and results.

There are many resources available in the marketplace that you can have in your toolkit. I have some I'll recommend throughout this book that I use in my practice and provide the reasons I do.

As a talent management practitioner, you can also use this list to assess your knowledge of why these tools should be used. Consider it a practitioner's competency checklist.

As a reminder, these tools are just that – they serve in the execution of the overall talent management needs and strategy, philosophy, processes and practice. They are not the ends in and of themselves.

For example, many practitioners are huge fans of certain assessments. I sure am and use them as a standard part of my practice. However, I combine their use with common sense, additional information about a situation and the parties involved for relevant context. There is no one-size-fits-all approach to Talent Management. And some are so evangelist about a certain product, they become hyper focused on that one product or service.

My recommendation, "Date the tools, be married to the overall outcomes you're trying to achieve."

Suggestions For Your Toolkit | What would you add?

- Employee survey tools (e.g. Survey Monkey)

- 360-Degree survey tools

- Assessments – behavioral, emotional intelligence, job relevant skills

- Coaching / mentoring

- Interview approaches – behavioral, emotional intelligence, team interviewing

- Performance/talent management software (that also provide data)

- Hiring support – background checks, recruiting firms, on line candidate sourcing

- Employee learning resources – onsite, online, mobile, workshops, webinars, e-learning, apps

- Competency models

- Reward programs and resources

- On line Collaboration tools

- Social media

- Special benefits

- Trusted Advisor

How To Use This List

This toolkit list is similar in use to the talent management map you reviewed earlier. Take the time to ask these questions:

1>...What do I know about each of these? *(Again, this list is also a knowledge competency list. The answer to this question is critical. You can't make effective decisions or make a case for its use if you don't have knowledge about their use* and value. *And, to help you out in this area, later you'll learn how to calculate value.)*

2>...Are there any of these we currently use that need to be reevaluated or its vendors reviewed?

3>...In what order are these most useful to our current needs? (Another way to frame this question: What people management challenges will these tools help us to successfully address?)

4>...Why? (This needs to be answered by you so that you can explain and make a case to other key decision-makers. Remember, if you're an HR professional, you *are* the internal consultant!

What can I do now to incorporate at least one new tool into my toolkit?

These are just a few questions to get you started. There's a lot of value to this exercise. Your answers and how you respond to them can make all the difference to your company and career!

Notes ✐

|> SHIFT #7
Effective talent management has an enhanced onboarding approach that includes immediate, targeted employee training and development

You'll notice on the holistic talent management map in the Onboarding Section an asterisk by the element 'individual employee competencies'. Read on to find out what that's all about.

Are You Complicating Your Employee Training Decisions?
I've been around the block a few times when it comes to employee training. As I mentioned earlier, I've conducted several thousand professional development seminars throughout North America over the past few decades.

Here's a key conclusion I've drawn: **We over-complicate employee training and development and therefore waste a tremendous amount of time and money.** I believe there are several reasons why. For now, I'd like to present a simple perspective on how to view and make decisions regarding basic employee training.

Before I do, I want to quickly make the distinction between training and development – an important distinction decision-makers desperately need to make. In most cases, I've experienced that when people use the word "training" what they *really mean* is the act of learning, or taking in new information.

What they *really want* or might be hoping for is <u>development</u> - skill acquisition and behavior change. We all know that **learning about a skill does not a skill make.** That's why making this distinction as we plan our talent training and development strategy and spend our precious dollars is so important! So as you continue reading, I'll be making that distinction by referencing employee training as *learning seminars.*

The Simple Perspective

I've spent many years working with a national public seminar company delivering many different workshops and keynotes on a variety of topics. During the course of my time with the seminar company, I came to realize that related to key soft skills in the context of work performance, no matter what the topic was, it all came down to just a few key themes. Additionally, a lot of the essential content could be repeated no matter the topic.

So, in working with private clients both in delivering learning seminars and one/one performance coaching, I've come to the conclusion that there are in fact **basic individual employee (individual contributor) competencies** that should be a fundamental part of every company's employee training/learning plan.

I'd like to present them via four questions and then recommend the behavior theme and corresponding learning seminar. In some cases, the theme and the learning seminar topic are the same.

Also note, when I talk with new clients about what training and development needs they have, in many cases they "mis-diagnose" the need. For example, there may be problems with communication, but the real issue might be emotional intelligence. So use these 5 questions as a way to assess your own "diagnostic" insights.

5 Questions For Assessing
Individual Contributor Training Needs

As you read through this **the =>** points to the topic or seminar theme

1). Can and in what way (style, attitudes, behavior) will they do their job? Will they get the desired results? –

Need:
>execute key deliverables in the time allotted
>driven by how they think and behave

Individual Contributor competencies: behavior theme and learning seminar topic:

Need:
>Self management, personal motivation
>=> emotional intelligence (EQ)
>
>Getting results/desired outcomes
>=> time & productivity management
>
>Ownership of work product, personal commitment to engagement
>=> personal/professional branding
>
>Ability to learn, think, problem solve
>=> creative, innovative, critical thinking
>
>Communicate in the written word
>=> business writing

2). Can they work effectively with others?

Need:
>Understanding, respecting and learning to work with different work styles, personalities
>=> emotional intelligence, team collaboration
>
>Rapport & relating style
>=> communication

3). Can they be lead? (an element of #2)

Need:
>In other words can they work well with authority / leadership - relationship to authority

=> EQ (emotional intelligence)

4). Can they and are they willing to add value in ways beyond their job description?

> **Need:**
> Personal values
> => personal/professional branding
>
> Situational leadership
> => holistic leadership, EQ

In summary, beyond the question, "Is someone capable of doing a job based on executing the functions of the job?" you can see that success in any role (even at the management level) can be broken down to (assuming they are the right fit for the job)...

"Can I and am I willing to manage myself to get results and can I and am I willing to work constructively with others? ...and do I know how to...?"

In my experience I am completely convinced that setting performance expectations during the onboarding period through key, *required* learning seminars can help to minimize a lot of employee management challenges and provide a baseline of support for coaching and managing that supervisors/managers greatly need.

In summary, if you had to choose what learning seminars on which to spend your precious budget, here's what I've concluded, considering the answers from the questions above:

1. Personal - Professional Branding => Ownership, engagement, personal empowerment, individual leadership

2. Time & Productivity Management => Get it done, get results

3. Emotional Intelligence => Work effectively with others, can be managed, lead

4. Team Collaboration (aka team building – not a great description) => Work effectively with different work styles/personalities

5. Creative & Critical Thinking => Learning to think in general generate idea, solutions, assess, problem solve, process improve.

6. Business writing => Written communication

Now, no matter what the creative title is of a seminar or workshop (and there are many out there - seminar companies are experts at that for marketing purposes), these core learning seminars represent development needs that inform participants how to and set expectation for:

> Self manage, self motivate, take ownership
> Manage time to get results and learn to be the most productive
> Work collaboratively and constructively with others, which includes working appropriately with authority and as well as peers
> Learn to think and problem solve (this is an ownership element as well)
> Communicate effectively in writing

I encourage you to review your employee training philosophy, expectations and planning from a fresh perspective using this information as a baseline and in that consider the following action items:

1. Consider the concept of individual employee (individual contributor) core competencies. What behaviors and attitudes do you want as a performance baseline for every employee?

2. Review your decisions regarding any employee training you've done over the past year, particularly what topics were chosen. Compare those to the suggested core employee competency themes.

3. Look at where your training dollars are going - how have they been spent? (Particularly as it relates to performance needs of your employees)

4. Remember, learning is just the beginning. The real training occurs when the information is applied and new behaviors are created prompted from what's been learned. Therefore, there must be accountability in place via a follow up or application plan. More specifically, the integration of the information needs to be tied into performance management and ultimately the business strategy.

Our Second Meeting

It's a beautiful fall afternoon when we meet again. This time I requested we meet outside the office to facilitate a relaxed, uninterrupted meeting.

You settle into your chair, organizing many pages of handwritten notes on the meeting table. You have an energetic look as you enthusiastically greet me and offer to begin.

Without me saying a word, you begin to divulge not only the answers to the questions, but significant revelations you've derived from the exercise.

You express that you've began to see the people side of the business in a whole new way, and have identified many elements on the talent management map that you've never considered.

I interrupt and ask, "Is there anything you discovered that provided clues as to why that young lady left?"

With great satisfaction you reply, "Well...this map and the relating questions prompted me to find out what happened with her. I learned that she had become bored and there was not enough challenge to the work to keep her engaged and satisfied, so she left."

"If I had been using this map, I would have directed our leadership group to develop some engagement and retention initiatives. I didn't realize something so simple could have potentially kept her here longer. I can tell you for certain that I will never let our talent walk out the door - at least without a fight!"

"Wow!" I proclaimed, "I think we have a talent management convert on our hands!"

"It all makes so much sense...if I'd only known earlier."

You continue on, disclosing additional answers, insights and discoveries.

As you come to a close, I ask, "Can you imagine the results of this exercise when your entire leadership team completes it?"

"You know, initially I felt uncertain and uncomfortable with the prospect of my team working through this. But, now I see it as imperative."

"Well," I reply, "Our next step is to facilitate a discussion with their answers. It sounds as if you're ready for it!"

"Absolutely," you assert. "It's time to get on the 'great' track. There are so many talent management essentials I need to implement."

"Let me assure you that you're already on the great track. Let's just keep it going!" And with that, we quickly schedule our next meeting.

I walk away from the coffee shop thinking what a wonderful experience, witnessing the shifts. So far they've come in sizes big and small – each meaningful in their own way and each serving the other.

I know that in order for your vision to be achieved, we still have a ways to go. There are many shifts yet to occur by many more people.

If we lay a solid foundation with you as the key influencer, shoring up your leadership, understanding and conviction, that will enable the next stage to be equally successful.

You were right – a different company will require a different leader and you are becoming just that.

Let's take a break from the story. I wanted it to serve as a realistic representation of an initial experience and conversation any business owner or key decision-maker would have when assessing talent management and its relationship to business operations and outcomes.

> **Essential Point:** Thorough, honest conversations generate the foundational *shifts* absolutely necessary to make meaningful changes. That's why *trusted advisor* is on the list of toolkit resources.

So, we've told a story and provided some initial assessment resources including the Holistic Talent Management Map™.

Now it's time to describe exactly what we're mean when using the words 'talent management', and additionally, what makes it holistic.

Section II
What is talent management?

What is Talent Management?

Let's give more shape and definition to the words talent management. I think it's defined and seen differently by many and that's one of the reasons you were asked to define it in the initial audit questions.

I came across what I believe to be the best and most succinct definition and explanation of talent management from Dr. John Sullivan, the former Chief Talent Officer for Agilent Technologies. His article entitled *Talent Management Defined: Is It a Buzzword or a Major Breakthrough?* provides what I believe is a comprehensive and practical overview of the topic.

He writes...

"Talent management is the integrated process of ensuring that an organization has a continuous supply of highly productive individuals in the right job, at the right time.

Rather than a one-time event, talent management is a continuous process that plans talent needs, which includes the following:
- ✓ Builds an image to attract the very best
- ✓ Ensures that new hires are immediately productive
- ✓ Helps to retain the very best
- ✓ Facilitates the continuous movement of talent to where it can have the most impact within the organization

The goal of the talent management process is to increase overall workforce productivity through the improved attraction, retention, and utilization of talent. The talent management strategy is superior not just because it focuses on productivity, but also because it is forward looking and proactive, which means that the organization is continuously seeking out talent and opportunities to better utilize that talent.

It produces excellent results because it overcomes the major problem of connecting traditional hiring practices with key business strategy. It integrates the previously independent functions of recruiting, retention, workforce planning, employment branding, metrics, orientation and redeployment into a seamless process with the broader view of company profitability; in essence unifying the approach to people management that produces significantly higher business results."

Dr. Sullivan enhances that definition by sharing four key factors that make approaching managing employees from a talent management mindset unique and profitable.

1. It takes an integrated approach within HR.
2. It integrates people processes into standard business processes.
3. It shifts responsibility to managers (and this is what makes our work distinct) for executing people management
4. It measures success with productivity that impacts profits.

The Role of Leadership & Management

In reviewing the list of the four elements, I'd like to zero in on the third for a moment. One of the substantial changes in this human capital management approach is to shift some of responsibilities to those who are in daily contact and have the most influence over the talent - the managers. In doing so, it calls for a more collaborative relationship between HR, front-line and mid-level managers as guided by the "C-suite".

It also calls for a change in how managers see their roles and how their individual success and that of their teams are defined. It additionally requires that managers integrate the second of the four elements into their roles as well. Dr. Sullivan described it this way:

"Talent management starts with the premise that managing talent is an essential part of any businesses success, where it is considered at least as important as budgeting, quality control, and customer service.

When talent management (people management processes) is embedded into standard business processes, you force line managers to think of recruiting, retention, development, etc. as *essential activities* that make a significant contribution to any manager's business results and success. By eliminating the premise that recruiting and retention efforts are "occasional" events, you get managers to begin to think that people management activities are not separate and distinct things that you do on an occasional basis, but rather continuous activities that must be carried out every day on an ongoing basis.

This approach to talent management provides managers with a convincing business case that demonstrates how their individual success is tied to the continuous process of recruiting, retaining, moving and developing talent. Once managers begin to realize that they cannot reach their output goals without effective talent management/people processes, they then commit more of their own time and resources into the recruiting, development, and retention of their talent."

For this to be achieved, a shift in management and leadership philosophy and the culture of a company is required.

The Best News In This Approach
Profits! It just makes sense that approaching employee management in this way will more effectively leverage all internal resources and facilitate increased profitability. That is reflected in #4 above.

Dr. Sullivan describes it this way...

"The final differentiator between talent management and standard HR is how the success of people management is measured. While most HR functions measure their success with functional metrics like number of hires, number of development programs offered, and customer satisfaction, talent management instead measures its success by assessing its overall business impact. Business impact in this case is measured by the overall increase in the productivity of the workforce (employees) at a particular firm. *In other words, you don't improve development, recruiting, or retention just to improve them; instead you improve these people processes in order to increase the output of your workers.*

The ultimate measure of effective talent management is the change in the return on investment for people management as measured by the ratio between dollars spent on employees (total employee costs) and *the dollar value of the employees output* (output value or revenue)."

Other Key Considerations of Talent Management

There are additional elements Dr. Sullivan suggests. Again read the article for the complete report. Under this category I wanted to highlight several from the list of other considerations that address our work.

- ✓ *A focus on high impact positions.* A talent management strategy requires managers and HR to determine which jobs, when filled with top talent, have the largest impact on a firm's success.

- ✓ *Accountability.* Talent management assigns responsibility for managing the talent inventory to the chief talent officer, who is responsible for results, not effort.

- ✓ *Rewards and metrics.* Talent management builds cooperation and integration between previously independent efforts through its heavy use of common goals, metrics and rewards. As a result, no independent function can be considered successful unless the overall talent management effort is also successful.

- ✓ *Balanced metrics.* Talent management gets managers'

attention by instituting a system of measures and rewards that ensures every manager is recognized and rewarded for excellence in people management (high workforce productivity). It simultaneously measures employee engagement to ensure that managers reach their productivity goals while using the appropriate management behaviors (two-way communications, empowerment, meritocracy, etc.).

✓ *Anticipation.* While traditional recruiting and retention tend to be reactive, talent management is forward looking. It forecasts and alerts managers about upcoming problems and opportunities. It encourages managers to act before the need arises in talent management issues.

The article also identifies practitioners and provides a very thorough list of elements to the talent management process, which parallels much of the lists you've already worked through. Check out the entire article at the link provided. It's a perfect compliment to this book, as written and shared by a leading CEO.

http://www.ere.net/2004/09/13/talent-management-defined-is-it-a-buzzword-or-a-major-breakthrough/

What Makes Talent Management Holistic?

When considering the summary of my experience as I've expressed earlier, the opportunity to get a bird's eye view of the complete operational needs of a company from the human capital perspective has been wonderful.

That perspective has shaped how I see and have defined talent when working with both individuals and companies. Because my view and experience has been so broad I see it more holistically – encompassing more than a traditional view.

My view combines the human side with the operational side. *Here are the elements that move it from traditional to holistic:*

1: A business approach sees and treats every employee as a whole human being; whole defined as mental, emotional, spiritual, and physical. That means taking into consideration their needs, and in that promoting good will, respect, and a commitment to their value.

There is a range of ways many companies are doing this - on both small budgets and large. With the emergence of wellness programs, creative incentives, emotional intelligence work, mindfulness and yoga classes offered on site, increased call for creative and innovative thinking, allowing prayer space, having onsite coaching or clergy visits and values-based leadership, it's clear that functioning holistically is increasing in its importance and it's also clear many companies are seeing the financial benefits to acknowledging and valuing the full humanness of their employees.

Companies who are practicing holistic talent management are experiencing better market position and profits. In reviewing the philosophy and practices of the Forbes - Best Companies to Work For list, you'll discover the philosophy and practice of honoring the whole of their employee's humanity is definitely demonstrated.

I'm encouraged as a proponent of this approach that it's not only the larger, more popular, cutting edge tech companies who do so this (like Apple, Google and Zappos) but – as an example – one that resided in a more traditional business sector - a grocery store based in upstate New York. Wegmans has made the list many times!

It's clear that holistic talent management is possible and profitable. The main thing that gets in the way is the thinking and personal values of a company's leadership. It must be a deeply held way of thinking and acting for it to be fully realized from the C-suite to Main Street.

Here's another example. In reading the book *Delivering Happiness* by Zappos CEO Tony Hsieh - it's clear his personal values include being a continuous learner, active in his community, and going the extra mile for the customer and employees. All of these are foundational to Zappos' success.

Hsieh's story reflects how those elements were demonstrated in his personal life, in both his thinking and decision-making. Those elements then, are reflected in the company culture he has formed and ultimately the valuation of his company when purchased by Amazon for $850 million dollars.

Did you catch that? Holistic talent management is profitable beyond the balance sheet. Along with a high company valuation, Zappos became an "employer of choice" in attracting the best talent.

As a leader or HR professional take note -- talent attracts talent.

2: The **second element** of holistic talent management is referenced above and comes from the comprehensive approach of **embedding traditional HR functions into the complete business process and strategy.** A lot of corporate energy is wasted when influential functions of HR and those who manage employees day-to-day are not appropriately integrated to maximize the capability of employees. This has been our reoccurring theme.

I've witnessed this lack of integration and collaboration particularly in the area of employee training. There is a substantial disconnect in how managers see their role and that of a training / HR department. It's clear that most managers don't see talent management as part of their job description and expect the HR department to "do the training" (which is neither logical or realistic). They expect someone to attend a training class and be ready to hit the ground running. *They don't realize that knowledge may be gained in a seminar or training class, but a skill is developed over a period of time.*

Without frontline managers understanding that training is managing and managing is training, there will continue to be lost opportunities to get the most out of and fully engage team members. This knowledge and practice deficit contributes to our apparent ongoing challenge with employee engagement.

3: Also included in holistic talent management is a commitment to developing skilled managers and leaders. What's the point in putting in so much effort, time, and financial resources to attract and hire the best talent when those who are managing them don't know how to successfully do so? **(I consider this a shift, though I didn't formally post it as one.)**

Therefore, management and leadership development is also included in the business strategy. It's not optional. It's seen as essential to serving clients, enhancing the brand, attracting and retaining talent and ultimately increasing profits.

Most decision-makers don't realize that not investing in management and leadership development will cost a company one way or another.

Additionally, management and leadership development is not conducted ad hoc, but is strategic in its design and integrated in its approach. It's thoughtfully created and developed around pre-determined competencies both broad and specific.

Broad competencies, for example, are those for managers such as emotional intelligence, decision-making, team management, coaching, personal productivity, creative/innovative thinking and collective productivity, to name a few. Competencies, more specific, could also be related to a manager in a certain context such as sales.

To accomplish this, our view of holistic talent management goes beyond traditional training/learning delivery models. It takes into account that if behavior is going to change it should be approached from an inside-out perspective; one that seeks to respectfully engage the will, spirit, emotions, and mind of a person. This is referenced in several of the shifts regarding employee training.

Additionally, talent management takes into account core adult learning principles that structure learning in a realistic, meaningful way - in a way that is easy to access, easy to use, has real-time relevance and ideally integrated into day-to-day experiences.

SIDE BAR
The 4 Key Principles of Adult Learning - The Reality of Adult Learning

Ever wondered what it takes to effectively help adults learn and translate what they've learned into meaningful behavior? It's been said many times that kids learn quicker and easier than adults and in my experience I've seen this to be true. They are sponges, absorbing everything around them – good or bad!

Children model and imitate behavior fluidly with little filtering...they haven't developed a strong ability to pick and choose which behaviors to hold on to and which should be avoided.

As adults, we develop filters or biases from previous learning and experiences. Anything new we are exposed to actually goes through those filters both on a conscious and unconscious level. Those filters can be both useful and not so useful, depending on the outcomes we desire.

For example, let's say an employee has been working for a company for some time that discourages creative thinking to the point that she is penalized when she presents an idea. On a subconscious level, the message she is receiving is that creative thinking is not useful or it's bad.

Now let's imagine that this employee has recently moved into a new career with a progressive, forward thinking company and is committed to using the intellectual capital of its employees and encourages creative thinking. How will this new employee behave? She may have some initial struggles allowing herself to be creative. Why? Because she has an internal, subconscious filter that tells her offering ideas is bad.

In addition to filters, as we age, unless there is a concerted effort to keep our brains alive and functioning at a high capacity, our brains go flat... they actually under-function. Critical thinking skills go by the wayside, and generating ideas become almost nonexistent.

Why does this matter in staff development?

Hopefully, you're already answering this question. If you look at the most common approaches to how employees are trained (if they are at all...because believe it or not, there are still some companies that have *not* made the connection between staff training and development to profits), you'll see that in most cases the "throw it up against the wall and see if it sticks" approach is being used. Another term I use is the 'band-aid approach' – we've got a problem, so let's do a training class and that'll fix it!

Band-Aid thinking reflects a lack of understanding of what it takes for adults to not only learn, but to fully integrate new principles to the point of a new behavior, habit, or skill....or achieve what we call 'unconscious competence' (See the Change Management Diagram).

So what does it take for an adult to change behaviors?

There are several different approaches to adult behavior change, but in general most training follows a model going from conscious competence to subconscious competence.

To go from conscious competence (meaning we have to purposefully think and act out this new behavior we're trying to create) to subconscious competence (we don't have to think about it anymore because it has become so automatic and natural) takes, at its optimum, the incorporating of the four key adult learning principles in all staff training and development planning!

So, here they are... and as you read through these, apply them to your current staff training experience.

_ 1. Spaced Repetition

An adult needs to hear something six to eight times to get it (and you thought that was just your kids!). That's right - there must be repetition of concepts a minimum of six to eight times. This helps a concept to be integrated or installed on a subconscious level... so the principle can "come to mind" in situations where it can be applied.

In fact, the most powerful repetition is spaced... I hear, time elapses, I hear it again...

Of course most people have already experienced this.... As you read the following, can you actually hear the tunes in your head or see the picture?

--"Plop, plop, fizz, fizz – oh what a relief it is..."

--"Where's the beef?"

--"Have it your way"

--"I'm loving it"

--"Just do it"

I bet you could name the commercial or company those sayings or slogans represent...Why?...repetition!

_ 2. Real, felt pressure to change

The reality is that people are more likely to move away from pain... faster than they will move towards gain. So, in order for people to be motivated to actually learn – that is, take on and accept a concept – there has to be a *compelling reason* which creates the DESIRE to learn and apply it.

Please know that the level of pressure to change is directly related to the desire or motivation for learning and implementation!

I remember early on when the Microsoft Office products first came on the market. At that time I was working in accounting. Learning to use a spreadsheet became absolutely essential to executing my work.

Without it, I virtually couldn't do my job and would have been replaced by someone who could.

Do you think I experienced <u>real, felt pressure to change</u> – to learn and implement? Absolutely! And, I experienced a bonus in adult learning – there was ample opportunity for real-time application and lots of repetition!

I learned Microsoft Excel quickly and was grateful that I was able to. I also saw the great value in the use of the tool. I can't imagine working without spreadsheets today!

It's been my experience in training that IF (and that's the key word) people feel that the training and learning is ABSOLUTELY necessary to real situations that have impact, then there will be adequate motivation present to learn and implement. So the question is, "Where's the pressure and how much is there?"

_ 3. Real–time application

Once someone learns a principle to apply so that a new behavior can be created, there has to be a real situation in which they can apply it to – over and over again - until they understand it, get it, see the value in its use AND until it becomes automatic.

I once had the opportunity to take a desktop publishing class for a software program called PageMaker. My *intent* was to use it to publish corporate newsletters. The cost of the all-day class at that time was $500.00 at an off-site location.

It was a great class. The problem? When I got back to work I never had the opportunity to use what I had learned and guess what happened? Well, you know the phrase "use it or lose it"? That's exactly what happened to me! Five hundred bucks down the drain.

_ **4. There's got to be a strong W.I.I.F.M.**

Ever heard of this acronym? It's everyone's favorite broadcast radio station, "What's in it for me"... or in the lyrics of singing legend James Brown, "the big pay back!"

For adults to be truly motivated to learn, the other necessary component that absolutely needs to be present is a strong sense that something is in it for them - that in fact there will be a big pay off!

The bigger the payoff, the stronger the motivation to learn and apply.

Let's look back to my story about learning Excel. What was my payoff? Well, several things as I recall: a sense of competence, more efficiency, ease in accessing needed data... and of course the most significant - with the most sweeping consequence - keeping my job... now that's a serious W.I.I.F.M.

What essential conclusions can we make?

I'm sure by now you've drawn some conclusions about your current staff training, development strategy and the principles outlined above. But let's bring it on home:

• For the highest return-on-investment in staff training and development there needs to be training in place that includes repetition (ongoing access to the principles and information), appropriate timing of the learning for real-time application, a compelling reason for the training and a strong payoff for the employee. In the training world many people are calling this "just-in-time" learning.

- Random one-time training can waste precious training dollars. One "training class" is not adequate to measurably impact embedded long term behaviors or for that matter develop a significantly useful knowledge base.

- If it can't be applied immediately (or within a reasonable time frame) it will probably not be used and thus eventually forgotten.

- These principles ask us again to consider these questions when making decisions regarding employee training.

    1. What do I want them to learn?

    2. What do I want them to change?

    3. Is this a learning need or a development need or both?

There'll be more on this in Shift #9. For now here are some *additional considerations...*

Company culture becomes a learning culture

For the most effective training to occur, the training needs to be integrated into the company culture. All levels of leadership need to be involved, supporting it and *most importantly modeling it*! It becomes the way the company functions with their employees and external customers.

Performance management

Training needs to be included in performance management procedures currently in place. Do you currently have performance management in place? I know this sounds like a silly question, but I need to ask it since many companies still only function with the antiquated appraisal model of once a year, which is no performance management at all really.

Effective performance management is regular, ongoing accountability to the behaviors and goals that are being targeted in a supportive coaching environment, as it's naturally integrated into the everyday experience of the employee. The most effective approach is focusing on one behavior at a time.

> *"Your performance depends on your people. Select the best, train them and back them. When errors occur, give sharper guidance.*
> *If errors persist or if the fit feels wrong, help them move on.*
> *– Donald Rumsfeld*

Ok...let's take a breather. There's a lot to digest. I encourage you to take some time and reflect on what you've read and what you've learned thus far.

To help construct a meaningful summary, I've provided a list of insights to get you started. These insights could also be referred to as shifts.

Remember, this is a reference guide and handbook, so make sure to add your own. Take notes and discuss what you're learning.

Talent Management Insights
so far...

- Talent management is an integrated, collaborative practice between all leaders, managers and human resource representatives.

- Talent management is "employee engagement" management

- Effective talent management includes constructive exit strategies (ways of coaching out or firing).

- Using software to support and facilitate talent management plans and processes helps to create talent management habits and a sense of responsibility and ownership among all stakeholders resulting in a talent management culture.

- Effective talent management includes having data that allows you to see your talent pool from a variety of perspectives. You can't manage what you don't measure and you can't manage what you can't see (your talent management software and assessments should provide that).

- Includes retention strategies when promotion is not an option (e.g. different job titles, expanded responsibilities).

- Talent management involves "mining talent" – the exploration of interests and skills beyond a current job description (we tend to see people based on their job description, not the scope of talent and capabilities they may possess).

- Being an "employer of choice" means that the company branding is an element of the ability to attract talent.

Notes ✍

Company branding is a component of talent management

Successful Talent Management Questions

- Do people really want to work for my company: why or why not?

- Do people want to stay with my company?: why or why not?

- If why not -- what needs to be addressed?

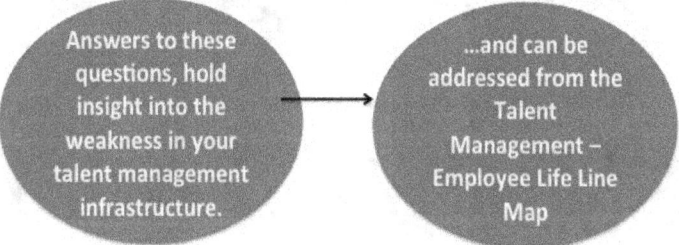

I don't know if I even need to comment on this one. I'll let the graphic stand on its own. But don't let the minimal comments minimize the importance of it!

Check out the 50 most desired companies to work for...

200,000 students surveyed

Source: http://www.businessinsider.com.au/most-attractive-companies-in-the-world-2013-9

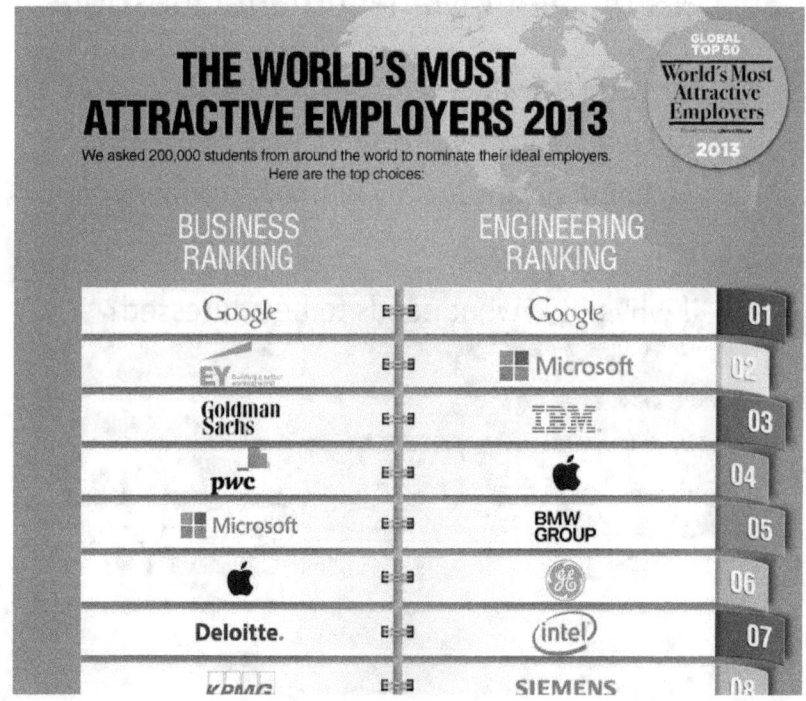

|> Shift #9
Employee training and development is misused and misunderstood, and therefore its use must be changed

"Talking about a skill, does not a skill make..."

I know we've already addressed employee training before this specific shift. The main reason I've done so is because it is an essential component of talent management and it is so broadly misunderstood and poorly implemented. The same attitudes, uses and money wasted are spilling over into the newer generation of HR professionals. I say, "Stop the madness!"

This section, therefore, is to spend a bit more time addressing the decision-making and to help you be more informed and discerning as you implement this element of your talent management strategy and build your infrastructure.

If I were to rename this section it would be titled: The Fundamentals of Learning – What Every Decision Maker Must Know to Make the Most of Their Training Dollars.

As I mentioned earlier, I think a lot of companies function under the old model of decision-making. You may have run across this, or you may have grown past this, but I have found this to be fairly popular today in the training environment.

The first problem is that people think one training session will fix everything. They may not say so consciously, but sometimes that's how decisions are made. "One training event will fix everything." I've got a challenging employee. Send them to a seminar. Then the assumption is that the behavior will actually change.

The next part of the old model of decision-making is that a couple of trainings per year is enough. For example, if a company wants to develop their managers or their leaders, a couple of webinars, seminars and e-learning sessions will do the trick.

Another one is "just because they hear it means I will get the results I'm looking for." Just because they hear it doesn't mean they're learning it or want to do anything with it.

Though someone would not admit this thinking consciously, the decision-making reflects it.

In reality, in order for every training dollar to be spent effectively, there needs to be these four essential components:
1.   Appropriate diagnosis
2.   Context, Desire, Willingness
3.   Consistency
4.   Continuity

Appropriate Diagnosis

I mentioned earlier the need to learn to diagnose and that when working with clients many see only the peripheral issues and therefore offer superficial solutions.

Unfortunately I believe seminar companies have trained decision-makers to apply solutions based on seminar topic titles. With that in mind many decision-makers will apply a "band-aid" to an issue when really surgery is needed. A band-aid in this case is represented by a seminar.

I believe many decision-makers are trying to shortcut the process because they don't understand that the financial investment needed for surgery in the long run will be much more cost-effective. Without the purchase of surgery, over time continuous band-aids will be applied, money spent and time wasted.

Here's an example of surgery versus a band-aid: You have a very disruptive, dysfunctional manager that is being sent to a seminar rather than the more impactful choice of receiving one on one coaching. Though initially more expensive, coaching more closely addresses specific outcomes, accelerate change while minimizing or the reducing the negative impact of the mangers behaviors. This has a much higher return on investment with a higher probability of achieving desired results.

I can state emphatically that for many situations I've encountered over the years, coaching (individual and/or group) should have been chosen over a workshop or seminar – or a combination of both.

Context, Desire, Willingness

What needs to be in place for the optimal learning conditions to occur? First, an employee who is learning must be consciously saying, "Yes, you know what? I basically understand that. I get it on some level." In order for them to "get it" on some level, they have to have a relevant context by which to apply the information to (e.g. something in their 'real' life).

Here's an example. My significant other is involved in an industry that I have no experience with. When he's explaining things about how to build a tower, or the presence of lead, or tax credits for old buildings, I don't know what the heck he's talking about. In fact, we've used the phrase "It's Greek to me." Same thing reversed, too. If I say I'm going to an ATD meeting or SHRM, he's thinking "What does that mean?" If fact, people have to have some sort of context by which to apply the information so it sticks. I call it the "flypaper and the fly." The flypaper's the context; the fly is the information, so that it sticks. We've got to say "I can relate."

What's next is that they've got to really want to learn. They have to really want to use the information and to use it now. I'm sure you've heard the old adage, "If you don't use it, you'll lose it." There's got to be an internal motivation and desire. As I just mentioned a few pages back we call it the w.i.i.f.m. or "what's in it for me?" That has to be one of the conditions that's present for optimal learning.

Finally, a person has to say, "You know what? I *will* work diligently to implement what I'm learning until I actually see a desired outcome. In fact, I'll *work through any resistance* until I get the desired results."

Here's what's interesting in learning... When people are experiencing new information, sometimes they experience both external resistance and internal resistance. The external resistance might be environmental. In a classic example, during seminars I teach about how to deal with unacceptable employee behavior, I give tips on how to coach employees. An individual in my seminar is probably thinking, "Well, I'm not sure if my direct report will approve of that, or if they'll get that." That's external resistance to the application of the information.

On the internal side, people don't realize there can be subconscious resistance to new information. Let's say a person is introduced to new behaviors related to leadership, or management. Their subconscious might fight it because it challenges a deeply held belief. That would make the application of that new information more difficult. The learner has to not only be aware, but also willing to push through those external and internal resistors in order to fully integrate what is being learned. The ability to accomplish this in many cases can be achieved through coaching.

In reality, all learning and training is self-directed, because the learner must be in a position where they want to consciously practice what they're learning, plan to implement it and embed it in their everyday work experience.

One of the least utilized and most effective contexts for learning and training is the actual real-life experience. Guess what? That's free.

The next thing that needs to be in place is that the learner has to revisit and consistently repeat what they're learning. In fact, they've got to be able to do so in a way that they're getting new lessons out of it, new awareness and a deeper understanding. That's all part of the integration and the application process.

Finally, the result of that will be going from conscious competence to unconscious competence. Another way of putting it is that the new behavior is so automatic I don't even have to think about it any more. We call that a habit or a skill. I ask this question in a lot of my seminars: "How many of you have ever driven home from work and wondered how you got there?" A lot of people raise their hand. I say, "Well, who drove you, besides five angels?" Part of that is the fact that they're so conscious at doing what they're doing so well that they've got back and forth to work without thinking about it.

What can we conclude?
1.   Just because someone has heard something doesn't mean that they'll remember it, or that they'll even want to.
2.   We can't assume that learners have a relevant context in which to apply information, and the fact that just because they hear it, it makes sense to them.
3.   We also can't assume that they will take it to heart, or that they're even willing to integrate it into their own lives.
4.   Also, we don't want to assume that there will be absolutely no resistance to the integration of what they've learned.

These are things that are often assumed in "training", but we've got to be aware of these as we're making decisions.

Here are some questions you want to ask yourself:
1.   When I make a decision on training, do I expect behavior change?
2.   Do I expect a cultural change within my organization, delivery of information for the sake of knowing, or is it a feel-good experience?

Those things are relevant. You have to decide what type of training am I deciding on, and what are the outcomes that I want to achieve?

You also want to ask yourself:
3.   What do I want to put in place to support the application?

If you don't put something in place, you will not be able to maximize the learning experience.

Here's my belief. Most of the money wasted in corporate training is wasted on the soft skill side, where it's not proprietary information. In soft skills training, we're wanting to learn all these behavioral skills and competencies to work better in the marketplace, work better with each other, to manage our time, be a more effective coach and leader, to collaborate better with colleagues, to get along – all of which are *developmental* in nature.

The key to effective skill development related to these types of behaviors is that optimal learning conditions must be in place. A one-time classroom event is not one of them.

There are a lot of different and more cost effective methods you can utilize to deliver information when you're just trying to push out knowledge (aka help employee learn) than classroom delivery.

In today's world, we're abound with technology, webinars, e-learning and mobile applications. I address these tools further in the section **Technology is a high-impact partner.**

At its core, you're asking yourself two things: Is this just about sharing information, or is this about developing a skill?

Skill development is not a one-time event.

Side Bar – The Reality of Change

To drive home the need to be more thoughtful in our decisions regarding training, I provided a diagram that maps what it takes to change – that is develop a new behavior. You could also say this is a map of how to *develop* a habit.

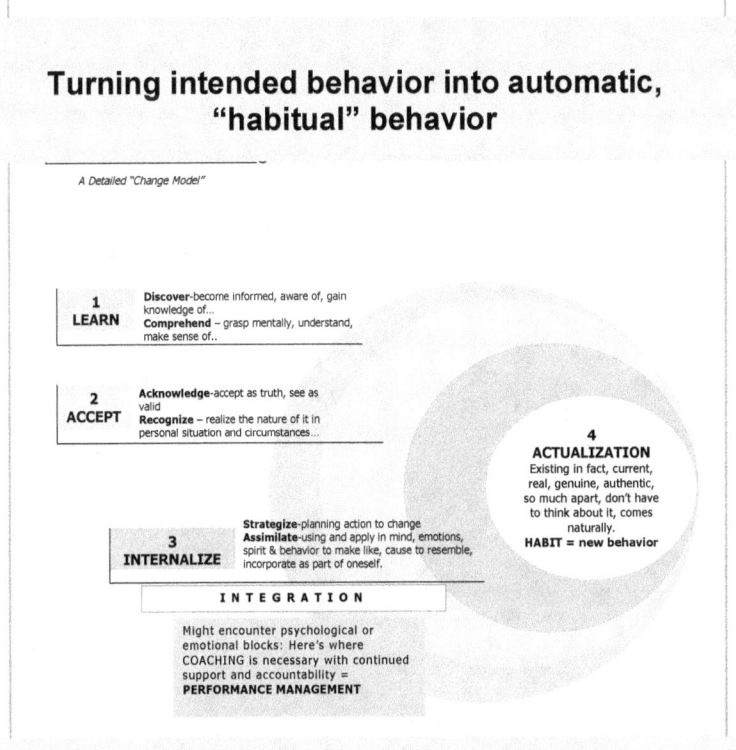

Turning intended behavior into automatic, "habitual" behavior

A Detailed "Change Model"

1 LEARN
Discover-become informed, aware of, gain knowledge of...
Comprehend – grasp mentally, understand, make sense of..

2 ACCEPT
Acknowledge-accept as truth, see as valid
Recognize – realize the nature of it in personal situation and circumstances...

3 INTERNALIZE
Strategize-planning action to change
Assimilate-using and apply in mind, emotions, spirit & behavior to make like, cause to resemble, incorporate as part of oneself.

INTEGRATION

Might encounter psychological or emotional blocks: Here's where COACHING is necessary with continued support and accountability =
PERFORMANCE MANAGEMENT

4 ACTUALIZATION
Existing in fact, current, real, genuine, authentic, so much apart, don't have to think about it, comes naturally.
HABIT = new behavior

Looking at this diagram, again consider these questions:
Is this training about learning information?
Learning how to do something (develop a skill)?
What new behaviors need to be developed?
Is it learning or is it developing?

Training as we use it, is not necessarily developing.

Notes ✐

|> Shift #10
Talent Management is about generating profitable behaviors.

"Always believe the behaviors over the words." – Oprah Winfrey

The Behavior of Business
Ultimately its all about behavior – business is about behavior. Company growth and profits are about employee performance; performance is about people – performance is behavior…business and profits are about behavior.

Business is really about three things…knowledge, behavior and resources. This may sound strange, but when you think about it, a business cannot exist without pertinent knowledge and behaviors that can leverage the resources.

So what's essential to the success of any company? A conscious determination of what knowledge, behaviors and resources are absolutely necessary (critical success factors) for that particular business to be successful. The behavior piece can be defined in two parts: functional job skills and behavioral competencies.

Behavior defined …
> the manner of conducting oneself: anything that an organism does involving action and response to stimulation: the response of an individual, group, or species to its environment having requisite or adequate ability or qualities.

A skill is the capability to do something well and is usually framed and needed in the context of a job description.

Example: Someone who can create a blueprint of a house.

A competency relates to qualities and capabilities beyond the job description. It reflects the make-up of the person in the job such as characteristics/traits, attitudes, beliefs, values, motives, character, emotional maturity, relational effectiveness and how those elements influence *how* a job is done.

Example: Emotional maturity to be self-motivated; able to efficiently organize and execute work.

Considering the information above, you can have two employees who are both skilled at drafting and yet one is much more productive (have overall better performance) than the other due to specific behavioral competencies.

In summary, WHO that person is on the inside, how he/she operates from within and how that impacts the way in which the job is done on the outside is a huge factor that lies outside the bounds of a resume.

Want to increase your revenue and competitiveness in the marketplace? Start focusing on the behaviors needed to get the desired results as well as the behaviors that are costing you. This is an essential talent management skill.

Behaviors help you make money or behaviors cost you money.

● ● ● Behavioral Costing

Cascio's Approach

o Focus on dollar value of behavioral outcomes in organizations.
o Do not focus on the value of the individual, but on the economic consequences of behavior.
o This is an expense model, not an asset model.

Source: Results Coaching 2003

It's all about behaviors. Note: You'll rarely find a list of competencies, such as "emotional maturity" on a job description.

In order for a business to stay competitive and profitable, three critical assessments need to be made:
1. A determination of those behaviors needed for the success of the business.
2. A determination of which contributors are in possession of those needed behaviors.
3. A effective plan to close the gap where needed...
   ...via training and coaching
   ...replacing a contributor with someone who is a better fit

This is the essence of effective people management. Awareness, understanding and focus beyond a person and more specifically on behaviors are capabilities every leader, manager and HR professionals must possess.

To highlight this point, let's look at some examples. As you read through these, try to identify key behaviors, consider the operational impact as well as financial cost. Also think about what behaviors could have been in place to mitigate the adverse outcomes or contributed to a constructive, positive outcome.

#1 The Gruff & Rough HR Manager
Linda is the key HR point-of-contact for all employees in a 125-person company. She is known to be efficient in executing all employee paperwork and keeping employee records in impeccable shape.

Unfortunately, she is also known to be impatient and insensitive in her relating style when employees come to the human resources department for help with issues concerning co-workers and direct reports.

Recently, an employee had a legitimate concern about being sexually harassed by her manager. It had gotten to the point where she was feeling very embarrassed and equally fearful of losing her job. The mounting pressure and anxiety she was experiencing was generating severe headaches resulting in sick days. Clearly it was getting to the point where she needed to reveal what was happening and get help. Yet, she kept putting it off.

Why? She knew that the person she would need to reveal this to was none other than the HR Manager who had a reputation for a lack of empathy and tact. This knowledge fueled the harassed employee's fear of bringing this critical situation to the appropriate authority figure.

In the end, the employee left and sued the company for sexual harassment, resulting in her winning a significant financial settlement, and the firing of the harassing manager.

#2 Entry Level Sales Employees
A promising, newly hired employee with a "go-getter" personality has been hired with high hopes of significantly increasing the revenue and addition of new customers.

Initially, this employee with a very outgoing personality was performing well and all looked good. However, as the next few months unfolded, his sales numbers started to decline.

His manager, who had been a successful self-starter and break out star with a similar personality type, could not understand what was going on. He had no clue how to help his potential star work through the slow down. The lack of insight into how people operate due to little management training left the situation floundering for both the manager and the new sales employee for the next several quarters.

Eventually, the sales manager became frustrated, which he found hard to constructively channel. His frustration came from two key places; the loss of sales revenue and his own sense of inadequacy in how to help this young "go-getter" regain his positive performance.

The increasing frustration began to erode the rapport between the manager and sales member and the rising star was transferred to a different role, which was not aligned with his potential. Eventually, he left the organization altogether.

The interesting part of this story is that the sales star ended up at another organization which happened to have an exemplary sales and management training program. He found his footing and became a consistently high performer.

Had the manager learned how to coach this high potential, he would have learned that beliefs impact behavior which equals results.

What came to light is the salesperson felt like asking for the sale in the style he was trained seemed too "pushy". If the manager had learned how to coach the salesperson by helping him reframe his beliefs and develop a more comfortable closing style, he could have made high sales again – all without leaving his position.

Questions: How could this have been handled differently? How could the manager have been coached to not loose this talented employee? How is this manager's inability to effectively coach impacting the profitability with other members of the sales team?

Assessment
*The ability to answer these questions by key leadership and those actively engaged in talent management is critical to the connection between behavior and profits.

This is the prelude to strategic training and development vs. uninformed and/or random training and development and ties back to the ability to diagnose.

Let's look at the HR Manager scenario. Here are some of questions:

- What behaviors on the part of the HR Manager contributed to this financial loss?
- What behaviors on the part of the harassing manager were involved?
- Who else might the manager been harassing and what kind of liability exposure has gone unreported?
- Where were the areas of financial loss in this story beyond the obvious of the settlement (e.g. sick days, lower productivity of the employee…etc.)?
- What would be the competencies needed (or "critical success factors") for an HR Manager to be effective?
- How would those competencies positively contribute to a company's bottom line?

Conclusion: The absence of needed relational skills and other behaviors had a meaningful impact on the company's bottom line. The irony? A minimal investment in management or executive coaching could have helped this key employee develop the sensitivity and relational skills needed to appropriately and adequately handle this legally volatile situation.

Additionally, had the HR Manager been more competent, she could have set up a coaching arrangement for the harassing manager and perhaps could have turned around the situation and appropriately coached the inappropriate, illegal behavior.

FYI

The average sexual harassment settlement ranges from 30,000 to 200,000+ depending if it goes to trial.

http://www.slate.com/articles/news_and_politics/explainer/2011/11/herman_cain_settlement_what_s_the_going_rate_for_sexual_harassment_claims_.html

A Few More Examples
#3 – Disrespectful, Abusive Boss

One behavior… a chain reaction
This example is quick, easy and
unfortunately all too common.

A lead supervisor is disrespectful to everyone on her team and abusive in the way she treats them.

Every time she has direct interaction with any member of her team it translates into that member being demotivated. Not only is the motivation of the employee diminished, so is the focus.

In this situation, it's common for employees to become distracted by discussing and complaining with fellow employees, which takes up work time, focus, and energy that could be spent getting accomplishing meaningful work.

It's clear that disrespectful, abusive behavior directly impacts the productivity of employees and creates a ripple effect to the customers and ultimately the bottom line.

Additionally, talented self-confident employees tend to have a low tolerance for this kind of behavior and their tenure will be short knowing they can be employed elsewhere in a better environment.

Additional costs to consider:
* Stress related absences
* Cost to conduct a search for those who have left
* Ramp up time for new employee to reach full productivity

For this example I must share a real story of the of the ripple effect of oppressive, uninformed management:

The scene: A manufacturing facility making a common product — potato chips.

The situation: A public relations nightmare.

This potato chip facility, with a headcount of 210 employees, had fired 58 in the first nine months of 1973 for disciplinary reasons. Morale was poisonous. Managers in the plant were frustrated, because, in spite of ceaseless disciplinary actions — written warnings, disciplinary suspensions without pay, terminations — employee misbehavior continued unabated. Workers in the plant, angry and resentful about the constant warnings and reprimands and discharges, sought any available means to strike back.

One ingenious worker discovered a cunning way to communicate his unhappiness with the way the plant's brass was running the place. He came to work one day armed with a felt-tipped pen.

He had discovered that it was possible to surreptitiously remove a potato chip from the conveyor belt that ran between the production and packaging areas, write a vulgar message on it, and replace it undetected. The vandalized potato chip would not be discovered until it was literally in the consumer's hands.

Word spread quickly among the employees about his unique trick for getting even with management for their harsh treatment of the hourly staff. Other workers joined in. Consumer complaints grew. Every day at the potato chip maker's corporate headquarters the mail brought more angry letters from customers, outraged at finding indecent love letters written on the potato chips they had bought.

What was causing all of the problems in this plant? On the surface, this plant seemed no different from any of the other 38 facilities that were operated around the country, making snack foods out of potatoes and corn. But at this plant the discipline system had simply run amok. As employee problems increased, supervisors took more disciplinary action. Harsher supervisory behavior led to increased employee mischief and misbehavior. Instead of producing solved problems and improved performance, more discipline simply generated more violations. The discipline system, intended to correct employee misbehavior, was in fact encouraging it. The traditional discipline system had failed.

Source: Dick Grote - Discipline Without Punishment

I'm sure you get the point, *but just in case...*

Here are additional examples of behaviors that directly impact a company's bottom line. Some of these listed are subtle, but when you really consider the ripple effect, it's eye-opening.

- Dominating relating style of a manager– not giving others a chance to contribute...I call that "leaving talent on the table"
- Resistance or refusal to learn something new and useful
- Blocked access to talent - employee difficult to approach due to abrasive and combative interpersonal style
- Adversely impact collaboration due to same behaviors
- A manager that has a hard time saying no to interruptions and there is reduced productivity due to focus disruption.
- Worker absenteeism due to difficult, disruptive co-workers gone unaddressed

Final Comments

Though the scenarios shared were leader based, the same holds true for individual contributors. The point is behaviors from any employee either constructively contribute to the greater good or they don't. We must become more *sensitive* and *responsive* to behaviors that are not supporting the outcomes we work so hard to achieve.

|> Shift #11
Talent Management is more than hiring for a job description

Best Hire – Best Fit
Selection, Promotion & Succession - Hiring Beyond the
Job Description

Holistic talent management hires from a view of best fit – the thinking is not necessarily *can* they do the job, but *are they a fit for the job?* There can be a big difference. You've gotten a glimpse of this philosophy from the previous shift, but it's so important, let's explore this more.

Ever heard of the book Good to Great by Jim Collins? If not, I highly recommend you read it. We support and espouse Jim's researched hiring philosophy of "getting the right people on the bus."

As a former recruiter, I spent much effort doing this for clients. I learned as I became more and more successful that the highest value I could bring in presenting candidates was finding the candidate that not only had the relevant skills, but one who would also fit beyond the job description.

So what does that mean? When looking at best fit – best hire, consider the following elements beyond a resume:

1. How will this person fit into the culture of the company?

2. How will this person fit within the team? (Team synergy enhances performance.)

3. What level of emotional intelligence has this person demonstrated up until now and how will that impact the group?

4. How will the current position for which they are being considered evolve and how might they respond (these days

many job roles are no longer static, but need to be responsive to the needs of the business)?

5. What are the key, **preferred behaviors** needed to be the best in this role (commonly known as competencies or critical success factors)?

#5 can really be considered the foundation of all the others.

Here's another way of looking at #5. I call it the "hand in glove" metaphor. The glove represents the job description, and the hand represents the way in which the job is done. You can have the same job description executed many different ways. The way in which the job is done is considered the competency.

As mentioned previously, a competency relates to the make-up of the person in the job (e.g. characteristics/traits, attitudes, beliefs, values, motives, character, emotional maturity, relational effectiveness) and how those elements influence how a job is done; for example: emotional maturity to be self-motivated; able to efficiently organize and execute work. Let's revisit the previous example in the context of hiring beyond the job description.

The job description of a draftsman: 2 employees both skilled at and certified in drafting and yet one may be more productive, be a better performer than the other due to the behavioral competency/skill of time management and personal discipline in his/her workstyle.

In summary, who that person is on the inside, how he/she operates from within and more importantly *how they prefer to operate or behave* will impact the way in which the job is done on the outside.

Best hire best fit then takes into account what behaviors / characteristics are most likely to contribute the highest level of success in a particular role and who has those in the most natural way as it relates to the role, the team and the company. It's considering the "whole" of a person for the full scope of needs. This certainly expands way beyond the resume and job description.

Two additional items of note:
1. Each element (competency/behavior/characteristic) impacts the profitability of a company.

2. You'll rarely find a list of competencies, such as "able to handle ambiguity" on a job description and yet it may be an important quality for a growing company with an evolving job description.

I've seen first hand the huge benefits of best fit hiring, which applies both in hiring, promotion and succession planning. In order to achieve this, companies need to put aside antiquated hiring practices, create a new, educated strategy and take advantage of the many wonderful tools available in the marketplace that can help those strategies be effectively executed.

Here are a few strategies to consider:

There are several ways to accomplish this. Here are a few:
1. Behavioral competency modeling
2. Behavioral interviewing
3. EQ interviewing
4. External selection assistance
5. Scientific pre-hire behavior assessments
6. Behavioral assessments job modeling
7. Best fit - job satisfaction, preference surveys
8. The Creative Interview Experience
9. Team interviewing

"Bad decisions made with good intentions, are still bad decisions."
- Jim Collins,

Section III

The Technologies of Talent Management Measuring, Validated Assessments & Software

"In business, the idea of measuring what you are doing, picking the measurements that count like customer satisfaction and performance... you thrive on that."
– Bill Gates

|> Shift # 12
Your talent management effectiveness can be measured - you can know how it's impacting your balance sheet.

I see a big disconnect with key decision makers between their desire to create and sustain a successful business and what it *really* takes on the human side of the business enterprise to do so.

This disconnect is the fundamental lack of knowledge of how people operate and the ripple effect of negative and or unproductive behaviors in teams that significantly undermine the profitability of a company. Or conversely the behaviors that are profitable.

Hopefully, the previous shifts created a practical awareness of this pervasive challenge. Equal to that knowledge is how to quantify the impact – what does that impact mean in real numbers.

It is my belief that *every* talent management practitioner, which includes HR professionals at any level and key decision-makers, need to be able to do this. Like bookkeepers that need to know basic accounts receivable and accounts payable to successfully execute the functions of their role, the same holds true for those who are responsible for talent management.

Can Behavior Be Measured?
Measuring & Cost - A Big Picture Example
Several years ago a study was conducted by The Future Foundation, the result of which was entitled *The Cost of Poor People Management*. 700 executives across the globe were surveyed. It included the countries of the United Kingdom, Sweden, the Netherlands, the United States, Hong Kong, India and Australia. Their polling put forth a series of fundamental questions about the philosophy of – and approaches to – people management.

Here are some findings related to the United States:

"Organizations in the U.S. are failing to actualize the latent human potential within their workforces and to address the performance issues hindering sustainable success. Indeed, poor people management is one of the worst hidden costs facing U.S. companies.

Overall, the U.S. is devoting $105 billion a year to correcting problems associated with poor hiring and people management practices. This shortfall is worth 1.05% of the total U.S. GDP. The reason for this loss of capital in the U.S., as uncovered in The Future Foundation study, is that businesses waste the talent and potential of their workforces and fail to match the right people to the right jobs.

The research reveals that an average of eight months is necessary to attain required on-the-job performance levels, which makes mismatches between person and job prove costly for both employees and their companies. Employees themselves are neither blind nor impervious to the demoralizing effects of poor people management practices. In fact, nearly a quarter (23%) of U.S. workers surveyed believe their colleagues are incompetent.

U.S. managers waste an average of 34 days per year dealing with underperformance. Senior executives claim they spend seven weeks a year -- or over an hour per day -- managing badly performing employees. More worrying still, U.S. employees admit that 68% of the mistakes they personally make never come to their managers' attention.

By not matching the right people with the right jobs, U.S. companies are also compromising the productivity of their experienced, well-paid managers, because their managerial time could be more productively spent on value-adding tasks. And the problems increase with organizational size. U.S. managers in larger organizations (>$8.5M in turnover) are spending 41 days, or eight weeks per year, on managing poor performers."

Source link: http://www.inc.com/articles/2004/12/karsh.html

I encourage you to read the entire article and report. It addresses many of the messages expressed in this book.

Know Your Numbers

As I mentioned at the start, one of the most important competencies any talent management practitioner could have is the ability to calculate costs associated with employee performance. Very few know how or a willing to do learn (I think it's a fundamental aversion to math, which I can totally relate to!)

This section is to help you get started. We'll work with a few popular scenarios and costs related to them. You'll discover as you we go along, that there are some consistent themes or costs in just about every scenario and therefore, most cost areas used in the calculations are pretty standard.

Additionally, in every scenario the ripple effect needs to be considered. When it comes to behavior most of the time, there will be a chain reaction effect, which broadens the financial impact. This is critical to consider as well!

As you consider the following examples (numbers are applied where available and applicable), begin to create you own templates. Customize them with the most applicable information from the examples. Or work through plugging in your own numbers.

EXAMPLE #1:   Disruptive employee or habitually underperforming employee

Impact => productivity
Management Decision: Kept on board, did not let go for a duration of one year. (This was a real situation from a manager I

coached. Some of the numbers taken from the Future Foundation study.)

Preliminary Cost:

a. **Time of Manager / Direct Report** - $60,000 annual salary / 40 hrs wk/ 50 wks a year (2 wks vacation)

$60,000 divided by 2,000 hrs of workable time = $30.00 /hr
According to study: 34 days a year = 6 weeks of work (8 hrs in a day) = 227 hours used addressing underperformance x $30.00/hr = $8,160.00 loss

b. **Lack of productivity of employee** - take hourly rate x hours lost

Earning of employee: $38,000 or approximately $19.00/hr
Assumption 1-2 hours a day of loss productivity - average 1.5 = $28.50 / day of wasted wages x 5 days; $142.05 x 4 wks = $570 /mth x 12 = $6,840.00

Total so far: $15,000

The Ripple Effect Cost:

c. **Impacted team member(s)** - @ $38,000 yearly salary
Determine impact time/hr follow the same as above - an hour

3 teams members 1 hr a day at the same hourly rate = (3 x $19)
3 hours a day loss productivity | 3 hours x $19/hr = $57.00
$57.00 x 15 hrs wk = $855.00 x 4wks = $3,420.00 x 12 months
=$41,040, cost per year.

Estimated Total from 1 underperforming / disruptive employee:
 Manager = $8,160.00
 The employee = $6,840.00
 Co-workers = $41,040.00
 Total Annual Cost: $41,040.00

In the spirit of a more comprehensive calculation, other areas should be considered. Start with the potential ripple effect to other departments and customers. I highly recommend when wanting to achieve a complete and comprehensive evaluation, create a "ripple effect map." That alone is eye-opening even before calculating the costs.

**Recommend action:
Create an "impact
or ripple effect map"**

Example #2: Calculating the value of a time management workshop

One of the most popular workshops I've taught across the country is *Organizational Strategies for the Overwhelmed* (I love that title!).

When I begin the workshop I usually go through a discussion of what the participants want to get out of the day. One of the most popular needs is dealing with unwanted interruptions from co-workers.

Though there are many ways to approach it, I give a four-step process that is tactful, respectful and easy to implement.

As I teach this, I ask them to calculate how much time would be saved (or as I say *recaptured for reallocation*) if the tip was implemented. People are amazed when they do the calculation beginning with a day, translating those numbers into a year at how much time is impacted and can be recaptured from implementing *just one tip*.

One participant indicated he would not only recapture that time, but also help other team members save time as well (the ripple effect). But for the sake of the exercise, we just worked his numbers.

Here's his numbers:
He indicated he would save on average 1 hour a day x 5 days in his work week = 5 hrs a week x 4 weeks = 20 hrs (that's 2.5 days for the month).

Over the course of one quarter? = 20 hrs a mth x 3 mths = 60 hrs 60 hours in a quarter x 4 quarters in a year = 240 hours

How many days is that? 8 hr. day = 240/8 = 30 days recaptured... **that's one *work month* and a week** *(25 work days)* **just from implementing that one tip!**

Now let's translate time saved into money. Let's say he is a salaried employee who earns $45,000 a year. Let's break down the numbers:

Yearly wages into hourly wages:
$45,000 / 12 = 3750 /mth / 4 week = 937.50 / 5 days = 187.50 / 8 hrs = $22.44 /hr

Estimated hours saved from successfully implementing tip: 30 days / 240 hours

240 hours x $22.44/hr = $5,386.00

Now let's say he works with 4 colleagues with the same wages and time savings. Same time savings = 240 x 4 = 960 hours to recapture. (By the way that is 120 days = 3 months of time to reallocate! That's an entire quarter of a year!!)

Same salary and time recapture = $5,386.00 x 4 co-workers = $21,544.

Total savings by using 1 tip with 5 employees:
    First employee - $5,396.00

Ripple effect = team members = $21,544.00
Total financial savings: $ 26, 930.00

Total <u>days</u> recaptured 30 + 120 = **150 days**

Imagine the numbers of an entire department or division with higher wage employees! And decision-makers balk at offering time management workshops because they "can't afford it." Really?!

When I get that response I know for a fact, they don't know their numbers.

I challenge you to take one of the earlier scenarios under the "behavior in business section", numbers from the Future Foundation Study or something from your current company and go through this exercise. It's truly eye-opening!

Example #3: Coaching
This is one of the most talked about areas of tracking return on investment (ROI). Coaching can be for any number of scenarios and employees, most popular are key managers and leaders.

Let's begin with a simple base formula:

Popular Formula:

$$\frac{\text{Client Results - Cost of Coaching}}{\text{Cost of Coaching}} \times 100\% = ROI$$

Assessing Results

I discovered great lists or guides on how to frame and calculate ROI. It begins by viewing these overall operational categories and then attaching dollar values to them and the outcomes. This is similar to the behavior in business section.

Sample areas of consideration Part 1:

Financial
   Increase in revenue / profitability
   Cost reduction
   Sustain revenue

Customer
   Retention = sustained profits
   Additional customer acquisition

Productivity
   Timely achievement of goals & objectives
   Motivation, engagement (saves on turnover costs)
   Targeted value activity

Employees
   Retention (saves on turnover costs)
   Work satisfaction & morale for self and others
   Improved performance reviews
   Promotion, succession, talent retention

Well-being (saves on missed days, productivity, team morale)
   Family support
   Savings on health benefits
   Fewer E.A.P. visits; absenteeism

Innovation - Creativity - Idea generation
   New products, profitable tweaks to existing products / services

Personal (motivation)

Improved Communication
    Productivity
    Motivation
    Increased speed to results

Effective decision-making
    Productivity
    Better results

Learning (knowledge value)

Minimizing counterproductive/sabotaging behavior
    Engagement impact

Assessing the Ripple Effect

Investing in coaching has a chain reaction. As a reminder, everything has a ripple effect. In the case of an executive, however, the effect is much more far reaching and usually with substantially greater consequences. For starters consider the following: the leadership team and whom they lead, departments, clients, customers, products and if publically traded, stockholders, brand identity... etc.

CALCULATION STEPS

1...Identify the immediate results, plus ripple effect:

Examples:
    > Star Salesperson increases revenue with 1 quarter of coaching
    > Executive improves communication to key team members *result* increased levels of trust = a costly mistake is caught earlier
    > Executive improves communication *result* valued leader decides to stay (no turnover costs)
    > Key leader improves his/her decision-making *result* action is taken quicker, team members have more trust in their leadership, productivity increases for everyone.

2....Estimate the % of value that can be directly attributed to the coaching experience.

> *An easy example:* Let's use the star salesperson: quarterly sales up $50,000. Let's say 90% of that increase was due to coaching = 90% = $40,000 direct gain from coaching.

3....Calculate and subtract the total cost of the executive coaching:

The coaching fees + the value of time away from the job of the person being coached *(some consider this part of the job and don't include this amount)* = Total Cost of Coaching

Example: Coaching $5,000 + cost of time away ($9,000 - Salary broken down to hourly $ Amount) = Total cost $14,000

Next: Subtract the total coaching cost: $14,000 from the value calculation (as above) $40,000 = Net return on investment = $36,000

For % calculation: Divide the return on investment amount, $36,000 by the coaching cost: $14,000 = 2.57 x 100 = 257%

In researching many reports on the ROI of coaching, the % of 257 is low. On average the return is reflected at five to seven times the initial investment. The return is generally high because coaching programs, unlike generic training is focused on specific needs, personal attention and targeting accountability.

Additionally, there is the consideration of the indirect and long-term value; there is in fact an undeniable ripple effective to coaching whether its sales professionals, leadership, executives or managers.

Also to be considered is group coaching. There is exponential value in that!

Improvements by % - Executive Coaching
The most popularly cited research regarding Executive Coaching is the Manchester Study. That study, as do many others, attribute improvement in a variety of areas as percentages. The key to meaningful ROI, however, is to translate those percentages into dollar amounts as we've done above.

To follow are examples of stated improvements by percentages.

Results of the study: Coaching programs delivered ROI *six times* the cost of coaching

Benefits to the companies were improvements in:
- Productivity 53%
- Quality 48%
- Customer Service 39%
- Reduced customer complaints 34%
- Retaining executives 32%
- Cost reductions 23%
- Bottom-line profitability 22%

Benefits to the executives were improved:
- Working relationships with direct reports 77%
- Working relationships with immediate supervisors 71%
- Teamwork 67%
- Working relationships with peers 63%
- Job satisfaction 61%
- Conflict reduction 52%
- Organizational commitment 44%
- Working relationships with clients 37%

Example #4 – The Impact on company stock price when investing in talent development

Laurie Bassi is the chairwoman and Daniel McMurrer is the chief research officer of Knowledge Asset Management, a money management firm in Bethesda, Maryland. Here is a commentary on the theme of stock price impact.

Title: Employees cost or profit source...invest in their development and see the results

"Managers are always claiming, "People are our most important asset." But deep down, they can't shake the feeling that employees are costs. Big costs. And they treat them that way. Quarterly earnings off? Cut the perks, rein in training, and downsize. This strategy may increase earnings in the short term, but it's myopic. Recent studies suggest that layoffs actually destroy shareholder value. And our research shows that treating employees like the assets they are—by investing in their development—boosts returns over the long term.

For years now, our research has measured the effect of spending on employee education and training—a "cost" that is buried in general and administrative expenses—on the stock prices of 575 publicly traded firms. We created four hypothetical portfolios (one each for years 1997 through 2000) consisting of between 20 and 40 companies that invested at roughly twice the industry norm in employee development in each of the previous years (1996 through 1999). We followed the performance of these portfolios through 2001. Their returns were robust and in line with a growing body of empirical research showing that organizations that make extraordinary investments in people often enjoy extraordinary performance on a variety of indicators, including shareholder return.

In December 2001, we decided to put our money where our research was and created a live portfolio of companies that spend aggressively on employee development. In its first 25 months since inception, that portfolio has outperformed the S&P 500 index by 4.6 percentage points (2.2% versus a decline of 2.4% for the index). In January 2003, we expanded our investment strategy by launching two additional live equity portfolios made up of similar development-oriented companies.

The results speak for themselves. While past performance is never a guarantee of future results, and while it is always possible to lose money, each of these three portfolios outperformed the S&P 500 by 17% to 35% in 2003.

Source: Harvard Business Review Online - 2004 | by Laurie Bassi and Daniel McMurrer

Source link: http://support.aspentech.com/supportpublictrain/HowIsYourReturnOnPeople.pdf

> Yes, talent management can actually increase the value of your company in terms of stock price, but also overall valuation – period.

Summary on Measuring & Costing

As with the coaching example, there are a few fundamental elements involved whenever calculating cost and this is particularly true with turnover. Below are some to consider. Again, I recommend you create a customized template specifically for your company.

Considerations:
Cost of Turnover = Separation Costs + Replacement Costs + Orientation-Training/Costs

Separation Costs:
1. Separation Pay: $?
2. Continued benefits contribution?
3. Unemployment Tax Impact:

Replacement Costs:
4. Communication of Vacancy - Ads, Electronic Recruiting & Posting,

5. Recruiting - Staffing Firm engagement
6. Pre-employment Admin
7. Selection Interviews (time spent = $ hourly value of hiring manager or HR professional)
8. (If hiring manager: time / cost = spent away from other productivity/key activities.

Exception: It's not a cost if company has an integrated talent management process, where talent acquisition is considered a regular part of the manager's job description and company practices = recruiting not a one time event in crisis, but an ongoing activity of looking for good people.

9. Testing – Fit for Duty Assessments (drug testing, background checks, best fit assessments)
10. Relocation Expense

Orientation / Training
($ amounts are samples)
1. Materials - Books $ 30
2. Equipment - Boots, uniform, technology
3. Formal Training
4. Training Wages
5. OJT Observation (ojt = on the job training)
6. Estimated ramp-up period to maximum productivity? *(generic estimate from the Future Foundation Study 6-8 months)*

Turnover Summary Totals
Cost of Turnover =
1. Separation Costs
2. Replacement Costs
3. Training Costs

Yearly Overall Cost of Turnover Summary
Estimated cost in your workforce annually (use your employee count and turnover #): Turnover Rate X Turnover Costs
Total Annual Cost:

|> Shift #13
There is science in talent management. Are you using it?

What Is Scientific Talent Management?
One of the most important and powerful tools to have in your talent management toolkit is scientific pre-hire, and best-fit behavior assessments.

Assessments that fall into this category are generally those that are EEOC compliant. Their compliance rests on a level of rigorous validation required which is the science of the tool.

The use of these tools in the arena of talent management leverages the science behind them and so we can say talent management can have a scientific component.

There are excellent tools on the market that are EEOC compliant (very few are by the way) and are amazingly spot on in identifying best-fit candidates.

Here is a link to learn about EEOC compliance: http://www.eeoc.gov/policy/docs/factemployment_procedures.ht ml

In summary, it means using assessments that are:

• Objective (developed and validated exclusively for use within occupational and organizational populations)

• Reliable (is proven to provide yield similar results if the same person takes it numerous times)

• Valid (it measures what it says it measures and is proven to be accurate—in this case, workplace behavior and performance)

• Neutral (regarding gender, race or age)

Of course in using a tool that includes the above, there are so many obvious benefits such as:

- It takes the guesswork out of knowing if a candidate is the right match for the position being recruited for.

- You no longer have to rely upon "massaged" resumes, hand-picked references or wondering if the candidate is really as good as their "sales pitch" makes them seem. Or, another way of putting its the candidate to meet the job posting requests...which be who they truly are.

- It can cause an otherwise inexperienced hiring manager to be effective in hitting the hiring bulls-eye (you don't have to be handicapped by the learning curve).

- The right behavioral assessment also gives you immediate data and insights into coaching and leading the team. That makes it easy to relate to and communicate with them in a way that taps into their natural, *predisposed, preferred behaviors* and internal, natural motivation (when you ignore the predisposed behaviors and motivations, performance is hampered to some degree.)

- It overrides any conscious or subconscious bias in candidate considerations for any talent management initiative, whether it's initial hiring, promotion or succession planning.

In fact one of my colleagues, Alan Allard feels so strongly about this, he wrote an interesting piece entitled, *Scientific Hiring or Gut Feel - Are You Willing To Bet Your Career On It?* In it, he makes some interesting arguments. Here is a portion of his article.

"As an HR professional or as a manager or executive, you know that the recruiting and hiring process takes an enormous amount of time and money and can make you want to pull your hair out. After all, if you hire the wrong person, what's that going to cost you in terms of your influence and reputation? And what is it going to cost your company in hard dollars?

According to the Labor Department, it costs on average, one-third of a new hire's annual salary to replace him or her—and obviously, those costs increase the higher up in the company the turnover occurs.

Now that we know the challenge, what are the solutions? One solution that more and more companies are using to find top talent, put them in the right spot and to keep them is what I call "Scientific Hiring." You might be wondering, "What the heck is that—and why should I care?" In part scientific hiring is about using behavioral assessments that are:

- Objective (developed and validated exclusively for use within occupational and organizational populations)
- Reliable (is proven to provide yield similar results if the same person takes it numerous times)
- Valid (it measures what it says it measures and is proven to be accurate—in this case, workplace behavior and performance)
- Neutral (regarding gender, race or age)

You might find all that interesting, but what does it really mean to you when it comes to making a huge mistake by hiring the wrong person? In short, it takes the guess work out of knowing if a candidate is the right match for the position you are recruiting for.

Not only that, you don't have to over-rely on your experience as an interviewer or on your gut feel—the two things many HR professionals and hiring managers take so much pride in. If you excel in these two areas—great—just don't stop there. Here's why:

A behavioral assessment will give you objective, reliable and validated behavioral metrics that are impossible to get any other way.

That's the science behind scientific hiring. You cannot and will not be able to get the information a behavioral assessment gives you no matter how experienced you are at interviewing or how much you trust your intuition or gut.

If you need to know if your candidate is *naturally disposed* to being a team player or detailed oriented or customer service oriented versus task and operationally oriented, you can't depend fully on a resume and answers to your trusted behavioral interviewing questions, etc.—as good as they are.

The fact is, too many HR professionals and hiring managers are over-confident about their track record in putting the right person in the right job. But don't take my word for it—take management guru Peter Drucker's word for it:

"...by and large, executives make poor promotion and staffing decisions. By all accounts, their batting average is no better than .333: at most one-third of such decisions turn out right; on-third are minimally effective; and one-third are outright failure. In no other area of management would we put up with such miserable performance." –Harvard Business Review

There are many reasons that explain why it's so hard to match the right person to the right job, but here are two:

_Many candidates are quite good at "selling" themselves in the interview.
_An "A" candidate in one company could easily become an average performer in yours.

In the face of what Drucker points out, how can you tip the scales in your favor when it comes to hiring the right candidate the first time around? (If you ace that, you will dramatically reduce your turnover, your recruiting and hiring costs and avoid a boatload of stress.) The answer -- put the science of behavioral assessments in your toolbox.

It's not about dismissing your ability to read a person in an interview or in how important your intuition is. It's about adding crucial information to what you can get from your gut or your people reading skills. It's about getting objective, reliable and valid insight and metrics that you cannot possibly get any other way—in short, it's about Scientific Hiring.

Without it, you are betting your reputation and career on how well your gut performs. If you listen to Drucker, you won't make that mistake." *(Learn more about Alan @ www.alanallard.com)*

> IMPACT INSIGHT: It's self-reporting and self-reflective - - the hiring authority has no involvement in the results.

As a former recruiter, one of Alan's points that deserve a side bar is the bullet point "neutral." I believe and have experienced tremendous intended and unintended bias in hiring. That bias can undermined our desire to hire the best candidate.

And as we've mentioned, an extremely useful remedy is to use an assessment. It's self-reporting and self-reflective -- the hiring authority has no involvement in the results.

I believe anyone who participates in any part of the interview/hiring process should be aware of how bias impacts "best hiring."

Additionally, if diversity and inclusion is a part of your corporate values, again, building awareness is critical. Consider the following article.

Is Bias Undermining Your Hiring?
I have to say, I've interviewed a lot of people in the course of my career. As a former recruiter for a growing Chicago INC 500 recruiting firm, I found myself interviewing people in my sleep! I did it so much, it got to the point that within a few minutes I could "read" someone and quickly determine if the candidate was the best fit for the role and client. At that time, one could say I was

very skilled interviewer.

I've also learned over the course of my professional development a great deal about how the mind works in the areas of perception and interpretation, both consciously and subconsciously. I've come to believe it's so critical to know, that I include it as foundational information in almost all my learning seminars.

There is absolutely no doubt that we all have a developed lens or filter by which we view and interpret every experience in life. **As interviewers, that lens or filter does not automatically and expertly turn off the moment we sit in front of a candidate.**

So what might be involved in interview bias? Well the HR Department of the University of North Carolina posted a list, which we all could learn from. Some of the elements are as follows:

First impression error
The interviewer makes snap judgments and lets his or her first impression (either positive or negative) cloud the entire interview. Example: Giving more credence to the fact that the candidate graduated from the interviewer's alma mater than to the applicant's knowledge, skills, or abilities are an example of the first-impression error.

Negative emphasis
Rejecting a candidate on the basis of a small amount of negative information. Research indicates that interviewers give unfavorable information roughly twice the weight of favorable information. Negative emphasis often happens when subjective factors like dress or nonverbal communication taint the interviewer's judgment.

Halo/Horn effect
The interviewer allows one strong point that he or she values highly to overshadow all other information. When this works in

the candidate's favor, it is called the halo effect. When it works in the opposition direction, with the interviewer judging the potential employee unfavorably in all areas on the basis of one trait, it is called the horn effect.

There are 10 in all and here is the link to the list -- it's worth your time to review and share with fellow hiring managers: http://www.uncsa.edu/humanresources/forms/InterviewerBiases.pdf

So here are a few questions that come to mind:
1. Do you have a sense of your own bias?

2. Within your company, is there any training with hiring managers in this regard, meaning is there procedure or protocol to address this.

3. Do you use other interviewing tools and practices to offset this? (Here's where the assessments come in!)

So, in answer to the question - Is Bias Undermining Your Hiring? -- the answer is yes! Even though I became very skilled at interviewing and finding really great candidates for my clients was bias involved? I would have to admit -- yes. Might I have presented different candidates if I was more bias aware. I'd say, "Yes," to that as well.

I've subsequently learned, skill in interviewing does not mean bias is not in play.

What's key is to build awareness and to consciously, take action to offset it! Where can we as a hiring community start? First, let's just be honest about it. Second, take the time to review this area for you and your company. Third, put in place a protocol, embedding into your hiring practices. And finally, supplement your hiring protocol with independent assessment tools.

Learn More: In my practice, we use several assessment tools depending on the need. When EEOC compliance is a factor, along with robust reporting we use PDA International. I've been exposed to many tools throughout the years of my practice (since 1998, phew!) and I have found this one to be one of the best. As a thank you for purchasing this book, I'd like to offer you the opportunity to experience this assessment at no cost.

Contact me at joann@thehumanpshere.com and include in the subject line: Complimentary Assessment

|> Shift #14
Technology is a high-impact partner.

Technology is essential in executing comprehensive talent management. Do me a favor, no do yourself a favor -- make your job easier! Please make this shift! Technology is a high-impact talent management partner!

There are 3 areas I'd like to highlight in this category:
1. Assessments – which we've already discussed and which is considered a technology
2. Employee training and development
3. Performance management / talent management software

Since we've already discussed #1, let's start with #2, training and development. This segment is discussed via two articles written during the launch of my mobile app.

Technology Area #2 – Employee Training & Development
Apps, Mobile, Social, Virtual

Part 1: The Employee Training Revolution Is Here – Don't Be Left Behind ...mobile and social learning are on the rise

Changing the Hands of Training
It's time to change "hands" – from the HR & Training Department and into the hands of the employee... out of the classroom and into the hands of your talent.

Ok...hold your horses... I'm not suggesting the elimination of these departments or classroom delivery. I am suggesting our role must evolve more into true facilitators of learning and engage **all** stakeholders in the ongoing process of training and development with the use of technology.

Yes, training and development is not a one-time event - it is an ongoing process. This is not happening in many organizations. And yes, we must include all stakeholders. That means changing how managers, supervisors, team leads and dare I say the "c-suite" are engaged in the planning and process of employee training and development. There needs to be a fundamental change in how they see their role, connecting their involvement to impacting the bottom line.

An emerging trend is showing itself to be a relevant tool to support this needed change. Going mobile is a valuable tool in the training/talent management toolkit and allows for all stake holders to participate in a variety of ways. It's both self-directive and collaborative as its facilitated by the employee training specialists.

Additionally, it naturally incorporates key adult learning principles. It's easy to use and has surprisingly affordable formats.

In this current economic climate, with so much restraint on training budgets, **now** is the perfect time to work with alternative modes of learning and training. The irony? The alternative may be **the most effective way** to get the results decision-makers want with the cost that anyone and any company can afford!

Consider this: Spend less and get higher return-on-investment!

Employee Training & Development
There's an APP for That
Use of a mobile application available on all platforms is one way that employees can have an engaging training & development experience. An application can house content and can be flexible in delivery and use.

An app can also be used as a connection to the larger community as a source for user-generated content, sharing best practices and obtaining real-time feedback. These are elements of the "social" aspect of employee learning. All of the major social media private group settings can be used, whether it's Twitter, LinkedIn, Facebook, Google+ or even YouTube. These are sources for 21st century learning, training, and employee development not usually considered.

This tool in particular helps *drive engagement* and helps develop learning rhythms that nurture measurable change and outcomes.

Additionally, for many users, you're not asking them to create a lot of new behaviors for usage. Many people are familiar with using apps and that usage is only growing.

A great example of the mobile revolution is demonstrated in this AT&T Commercial showing mobile sharing from a management, customer service and best practices solution: https://www.youtube.com/watch?v=Ilz6E540IRw

I know in the HR tech community, whose device to use is an ongoing challenge to address. For example, how do we accommodate "byod" practices (bring your own device) and still ensure security?

We are truly in the training wheels stage. But we've got to persevere! Mobile devices are here to stay and it's to our financial advantage to leverage them in all operational spaces.

Part 2: Are You Ready For An Employee Training Revolution?

Revolution Is A Powerful Word
Revolution is one powerful word. If you look at how that word has been manifested through-out history, the activity surrounding it has been undeniable.

One critical truth is employee training and development must change! Why? The reasons are listed below. It's what I've consistently heard over the years in my travels -- no matter what part of the country. I won't expound. I'll just state them as I've

heard them:
1. Corporate training on the whole *sucks!*
2. It's boring
3. I usually try to figure out a way to get out of it
4. It's too long
5. I wish I could get what I needed quicker, better, faster
6. What's the point?
7. I had to come
8. I was sent when the person who really needed to come is not here.
9. It's like torture sitting all day in a classroom

As a colleague, I sympathize. I've met many HR professionals who are swamped with little to no support. Often times, they're thrown into roles or have inherited sweeping responsibilities.

Here's the point - over the two decades that I've traveled, I've heard the same stories about training even with moderate developments in e-learning, webinars, etc.

All of this served to birth a desire in me to influence change in the industry and experience of the everyday employee.

So, What About The Revolution?
I checked out the meaning of revolution in Webster's Dictionary and below is part of that definition. Pay careful attention to it. It's clear from much of the language in the definition, that we are nowhere near a "revolution" in employee training.

a : a sudden, radical, or complete change

b : a fundamental change in political organization

c : activity or movement designed to effect fundamental changes in the socioeconomic situation

d : a fundamental change in the way of thinking about or visualizing something : a change of paradigm

e : a changeover in use or preference especially in technology <the computer *revolution*>

What's instructive here is to see clearly what a revolution should look like and what's really required. You could essentially replace the definition of revolution with a word in the title of this book, a *shift*.

The bottom line? Substantive change in how we must approach, view, and execute what we want to happen - even to the point where some might call it *radical*!

The good news is technology has advanced to the point where it can be a useful partner in this revolution!

Collectively, I hope all decision-makers are experiencing fundamental *shifts* in their beliefs that training employees, and training as we have known it **must change and that technology must play a substantial role in helping us.**

And finally, we must equip ourselves to participate in that change in our part of the universe, *providing the leadership so desperately needed* to make a difference for our profession, our internal and external customers, and our company's bottom line. I see basic technology knowledge as core competency for *every* HR professional! There can be no more, "Oh let the tech department do it!"

Newsflash – this is true for teachers as well. I've learned a lot from websites devoted to training teachers how to incorporate technology in their classrooms. Let it not be said that college grads are coming into companies that are behind in their use of technology! Not a way to attract talent - #justsayin.

I've diligently worked to teach myself about simple technologies and how they can be incorporated into the corporate learning experience. That research resulted in the purchase of an app platform that effortlessly accommodates them.

The exciting "ah ha" is that many of the simple technologies are free and available to anyone who chooses to use them for whatever they desire. And many are leveraging them to great benefit -- consider for example YouTube, the 3rd largest search engine on the web. There are people who've become millionaires by placing their content there. What does that tell us as teaching and training professionals? Videos are big!

My goal was to combine the mobile capability with simple technologies to provide very cost effective "just in time" learning offerings and additionally, if using an app was not desirable, translate those into virtual offerings. I wanted to give an enhanced meaning to "blended learning."

Benefits Of Certain App Solutions
Here's a list of the benefits I discovered in using an app as a training resource:

- Don't need to be bogged down with an LMS (learning management system)
- Can be used in any part of the world
- Doesn't take up server / bandwidth space
- Nimble design for evolving training needs
- Simple authoring tools
- User friendly design functionality - don't have to be a techie to use or administer
- Cost effective - very affordable
- Very accessible/usable training resource
- Highest return on investment with the integrated design for crowd-sourcing best practices, "just in time" learning & application, and maximizing the use of adult learning principles.
- Can have propriety company branded app for a nominal cost
- Does not require wireless access only, only a cell connection is necessary
- Can be a stand alone solution or can be easily incorporated with any blended learning-training strategy
- content provided or proprietary content can be

incorporated

Additionally, here is a list of the technologies that can be used in a virtual classroom or via an app.

- RSS feeds
  - ⇨ Short audios
  - ⇨ Short videos
  - ⇨ Learning links
  - ⇨ Podcasts
  - ⇨ Blog platforms

Of important note -- most of these are *free or low-cost*. They are *nimble* in delivery, and are easy authoring tools.

All in all, if an app is not a consideration for you, then at least make sure the website used for employee learning is mobile-friendly. Mobile friendly means that when accessed from a mobile device it conforms in view and function. It's easy to read and easy to navigate.

Technology Area #3: Performance Management Software

Imagine that with a wave of a magic wand you could push a button to get all sorts of stats and charts about your employees in an instant – right at your fingertips. *Information like....*

...Who needs help
...Who are your stars
...Who are your high potentials
...Who is hitting training and education goals
...Who is on their way out
...Who is coachable – and who's not

Well, you don't have to dream about it, there is software available that can do just that. As we've already stated, advances have made technology a significant talent management partner. And the good news is it's extremely affordable! That means the return on investment is so substantial every company can have it!

There is a breath of advantages to using this type of software. Here are just a few (and when you read this list, you can see why I started this section with "do me a favor, make your job easier!")

- Helps set and track clear expectations, goals, promotes focus to achieve more desired results
- Supports ongoing coaching – reminder of those goals, both formal and informal, encouragement, feedback, teaching, instructing
- Ties to business objectives
- Tracking/documenting by managers *and* team members (bonus=engagement tool!)
- Makes performance appraisals, reviews easier
- Helps create sounds talent management habits (it's as if the software is the coach)
- Provides a satisfying, *legal* process to coach out: documentation is provided by both the manager and employee
- Metrics, data for broad overview for effective strategic decision-making

When you consider the cost weighed against this list, frankly it's shocking just how few companies have this in place.

Here are just a couple of examples of data that can be used. Remember, data is your talent management partner, too!

Review the following chart. This is an example of a **9-box** chart used to assess the "state" of a talent pool. 9 Box charting is a popular talent management practice.

	Low	Moderate	High
High	"Rough Diamond" Low Performer/High Potential	"Future Star" Moderate Performer/High Potential	"Consistent Star" High Performer/High Potential
Moderate	"Inconsistent Player" Low Performer/Moderate Potential	"Key Player" Moderate Performer/Moderate Potential	"Current Star" High Performer/Moderate Potential
Low	"Talent Risk" Low Performer/Low Potential	"Solid Professional" Moderate Performer/Low Potential	"High Professional" High Performer/Low Potential

Potential Assessment ↑

Performance Assessment →

Here's how it's used - 9-Box Grid overview:

• The 9-box grid is a commonly used tool and framework to aid in a discussion of employee strengths, performance and development needs. It's a great resource of mapping how who or who might not be coachable.

• It is often used in a group setting. Managers collectively review current performance and future potential of a specific segment of their workforce. These multiple perspectives provide a balanced view of an employee's skills and growth areas.

• The grid can also be used as a planning tool by an individual manager.

• The 9-box grid is the end-product of a larger talent management
process and strategy in which leaders identity talent and organizational needs, critical job roles and capabilities.

• Proactive leaders use the outcome of a talent review (I call it "talent audit) to initiate development discussions, implement development plans that can also serve promotion and succession planning.

Q: How can the 9 Box grid help you?

Here's another example of a great technology tool!
Org Chart Software

It provides relevant information for any employee (with appropriate permissions) right at your fingertips. As the description suggests, you can see key information all in one view.

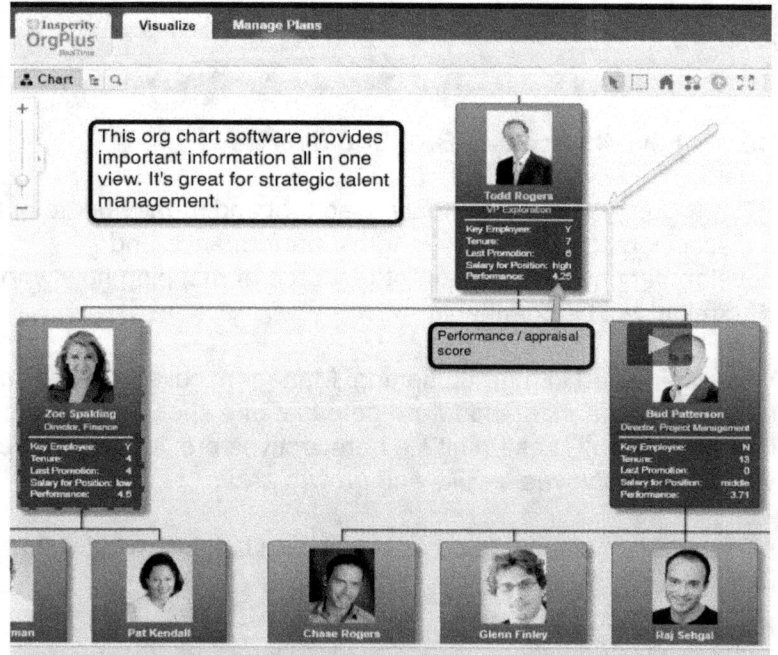

Source: Insperity - http://www.insperity.com/products/organizational-planning/orgplus-realtime/video-tour

Why These Tools Really Matter

I'll answer this question starting with a short anecdotal story. Ever heard of the Hawthorne Effect?

> In the late 1950s, the GE plant in Hawthorne, California brought in some consultants to measure the effect of brighter lighting on the productivity of their factory workers. The consultants first took productivity measurements to establish a baseline. Then they intensified the brightness of the lighting and measured again.
>
> Productivity increased.
>
> They increased the brightness even more and productivity went up again. After raising the brightness two more times, they saw two more increases in productivity. On a hunch, they lowered the lighting and measured one more time. Productivity went up!
>
> They figured out that the productivity gains were not related to the brightness of the lights, but to the act of measuring. They were paying a lot of attention to the effectiveness of their workers. And guess what? The workers responded by working more effectively.
>
> What do you pay a lot of attention to? What are you constantly

So why do these tools really matter? **We can't change what we don't know and can't see. These tools help us measure so that we *can* see.** Technology truly is an essential partner.

Do you have tools and resources in your toolkit to help you measure, providing you with critical data for the best possible decision-making? This is literally and in the most practical ways "managing your talent.

Notes ⟳

|> Shift #15
Getting help is only costly if you don't achieve your desired results.

You can't solve a problem at the same level of thinking at which you arrived at it. - Albert Einstein

Let's face it, for every moment you're not taking action on what's been presented, you're losing money. I am very confident that the information in this book will help your company save and make money through effective talent management.

The best way to quickly stop the financial bleed is to do two things:
> 1) Take action on what you can do now – start with something!
> 2) Get outside help

Throughout my career, I've had exceptional help in changing my results both personally and professionally. There are many times I knew what to do, but felt overwhelmed, didn't know where to start, carried some old thinking that clouded my judgment and decision-making as I was attempting to move forward and in summary just did not feel fully equipped.

We know that having an independent, educated perspective is one of the values of coaching. Discerning help provides useful input, insight and feedback. A respected colleague Betsy Jordan shares this with her clients, "Sometimes we really can't see the forest for the trees, so we need someone who is on a completely different tree!" This principle works in all aspects of business.

Help & Money

Let's also face the fact that there is an inherent fear in getting outside help, particularly when you have to pay for it. This fear primarily centers on wasting money and being taken advantage of.

Yet, if you want to quickly put your shifts into action and accelerate your implementation, the best decision you could make is to get help. It might mean acquiring a mentor or hiring a coach or consultant.

When you're paying for a coach or consultant, they can and should not only help with the assessing phase, but also make recommendations that get you results. *If you get the results you really want, you'll feel that the money invested was well spent.* An additional bonus?...the results will be reflected on your balance sheet.

Here's just a starter list of the benefits you can experience when obtaining outside help:
1. Your operational learning curve and those of your leadership team will be strategically shorted
2. Your company will make more money
3. Your leadership and management will quickly and substantially be enhanced (and those of your leadership team).
4. Your practical knowledge acquisition will be accelerated
5. You and your leadership team will save time
6. You, your company will save money
7. You'll make better decisions faster
8. Maximize existing human capital
9. Increased stakeholder buy-in
10. Enhance collaboration at multiple levels

A final thought – competent help might and in many cases will "feel" expensive, so here's a rule of thumb as shared by Betsy Jordan, *"What you spend should never be more expensive than what your challenges are costing you."* And as we know from the section on measuring – though they might be hidden, they surely are costing you!

So I'll reframe shift #12 – consider the money an investment in a partnership that will *drive a return.*

Your Summary
I thought it would be helpful to present all the shifts in one place. I recommend using it as a checklist for you and other decision-makers. It's a great resource to stimulate a conversation and to gauge where the work should be begin.

The 15 Shifts

Shift #1 - I can have Talent Management needs even if my company is doing well. My company can go from good to great or pain to recovery.

Shift #2 - How I see them and what I call them matters

Shift #3 - A different company will require different leadership. If I want my company to change, then I will need to change – first.

Shift #4 - Effective Talent Management can only be executed if all leadership is on board... and they too have made the shifts.

Shift #5 - Talent Management is a comprehensive integrated business strategy

Shift #6 - Talent Management requires a toolkit of resources to fulfill its objectives

Shift #7 - Effective talent management has an enhanced onboarding approach that includes immediate, targeted employee training and development

Shift #8 - Company branding is a component of talent management.

Shift #9 - Employee training and development is misused and misunderstood and therefore its use must be changed.

Shift #10 - Talent Management is about generating profitable behaviors

Shift #11 - Talent Management is more than hiring for a job description.

Shift #12 - My Talent Management effectiveness can be measured - I can know how it's impacting my balance sheet.

Shift #13 - There is science in Talent Management.
Am I using it?

Shift #14 - Technology is a high-impact partner.
It's essential in executing comprehensive talent management.

Shift #15 - Getting help is only costly if I don't achieve my desired results.

About the Author

JoAnn Corley is the founder and CEO of The Human Sphere™, a consultancy that helps companies increase profits through holistic talent management.

People have said about JoAnn that she is an emerging voice in the business marketplace...a catalyst for innovative thinking...passionate for bringing theory into reality in the laboratory of real life!

She brings fresh thinking that matches the realistic talent management needs of the 21st century workplace. She is known as a champion of human potential in the arena of business enterprise.

She is an experienced talent management specialist and a dynamic, inspiring speaker, author & coach. She has a contagious passion and energy for the topics she delivers, sharing that passion with thousands through-out North America specializing in seminars on effective management through coaching, time & organizational management, personal empowerment and branding, emotional intelligence, creative and innovative thinking, team collaboration and holistic talent management. She has the unique distinction of having conducted seminars in *every state in the U.S. and every major city.*

She is author of several books, Brain on Fire – How To Unleash Your Creative Superpowers, *The Force Within, Organizational Strategies for the Overwhelmed, How to Manage Your Time, Space, & Priorities to Work Smart, Get Results, & Be Happy,* Wisdom@Work and *The 1% Edge – Power Strategies to Increase Your Management Effectiveness.*

She is also contributing author to the book, Ordinary Women, Extraordinary Success, a collaborative effort with some of the top female motivational speakers in North American and hailed by Jack Canfield of Chicken Soup for the Soul fame as a must read.

Amazon Author page:
http://www.amazon.com/JoAnn-R.-Corley/e/B004HGQKZ2

JoAnn also has a unique passion for the connection of technology to enhance the quality of both one's personal and professional life. She sees herself as a "non-techie tech" that loves to learn about what's next. That interest lead to the development of her mobile learning-training app - The 1% Edge Portable Coach (available on all smartphone platforms).

She is known by her clients as insightful, passionate and an acute strategic thinker as she assists them in reaching their targeted outcomes.

Ms. Corley founded Convergence Consulting Group in 1998, a human resource-organizational development firm, which has provided services to a variety of industries such as; accounting & finance, engineering, government, staffing, risk management, not-for-profits, and sales to name a few. It has recently been re-named **The Human Sphere**™ to reflect expanded offerings under the umbrella of holistic talent management.

Prior to launching her consulting practice, she spent several years as the International Benefits Manager for a not-for-profit, then moved on to become a Senior Recruiter for a boutique, Chicago recruiting firm. She has worked for 2 INC 500 companies and has professional affiliations with ATD & SHRM.

Named to several top100 lists for most social HR experts to follow, you can find her on most social media platforms as well as radio shows and online media across the country and internationally. She has been quoted or featured in articles for NBC News, Monster.com, Harvard Business Review, HR Hero, ASTD National, Management Business Daily, to name a few, and has additionally served as North America Career Contributor for the Daily Telegraph UK.

Social Media | Additional Resources

I invite you to connect with me on social media and visit my website for additional resources to add to your toolkit.

Twitter
@joanncorley

Google+
https://plus.google.com/+JoAnnCorley

Facebook
https://www.facebook.com/joanncorley.the1percentcoach

LinkedIn
www.linkedin.com/in/joanncorley

Websites

Talent management blog:	www.joanncorleyspeaks.com
Company site:	www.thehumansphere.com
Professional development blog:	www.the1percentedge.com

Email: joann@thehumansphere.com

To order copies for your company with discount considerations, use the email above.

To get input on your talent management needs contact us at the company site above.

www.ingramcontent.com/pod-product-compliance
Lightning Source LLC
Chambersburg PA
CBHW072304200526
45168CB00014B/504